THE CHRISTIAN FAILURE

THE CHRISTIAN FAILURE

Ignace Lepp

Translated by Elizabeth Strakosch

1962

THE NEWMAN PRESS
Westminster: Maryland

First published as Le Monde Chretien
et Ses Malfaçons by Les Editions Aubier

© 1962 BLOOMSBURY PUBLISHING CO. LTD.

Nihil obstat: Joseph Can Cartmell, D.D., Ph.D.
                              Censor.

Imprimatur: Liverpolii, die 6 Februarii 1962
                    Antonius Bullen
                              Cancellarius.

The Nihil obstat and Imprimatur are official declarations
that a book is free of doctrinal or moral error. No implica-
tion is contained therein that those who have granted the
nihil obstat and imprimatur agree with the contents, opinions
or statements expressed.

Photographs reproduced by kind permission of
the Radio Times Hulton Picture Library
and of Ewing Galloway, U.S.A.

Made and Printed in Great Britain by C. Tinling & Co. Ltd.
Liverpool, London and Prescot.

CONTENTS

Many novelists both before and after Bernanos have taken priests for their heroes. Some have even succeeded quite well in conveying the drama of God's servants living in a world steadily moving away from God. I have no intention of either emending the works of the novelists or putting myself in the same category.

I lay no claim to having made an impartial study of the position in which priests find themselves in the modern world. I was called to the priesthood late in life after spending my youth in a world in which God had no place and there was nothing to enlighten my ignorance of religion, so it is only natural that I do not view the sacerdotal order and its duties from the same angle as those born and bred in a Christian atmosphere.

In my first book *From Karl Marx to Jesus Christ** I tried to report as faithfully as possible how it happened that I became a communist and a militant one and how disappointed I was when I came face to face with the reality of the system during my stay in the Soviet Union. I was swept into the Church of Christ on a wave of great enthusiasm and it seemed to me that at last I had found what, without knowing it, I had sought in vain in communism.

But gradually it dawned on me that the actual life of Catholics did not altogether conform to the idea I had conceived. I had been naive enough to believe that relations between Christians were a kind of pre-figuring of the kingdom of God. But I was to discover that a deep gulf separates the Church, the Mystical Body, from the Christian 'world'.

I do not expect—nor ever have expected—the Church to be a purely spiritual entity, because obviously she must be endowed with a body in order to enable her mission in time and

* Sheed and Ward, London, 1958.

space, here on earth, to be accomplished. Moreover since this body must be composed of material elements supplied by the world I was never shocked to find that the Church has institutions like those of other human societies and has her own officials and laws. And no one other than a pharisee could be scandalised by the imperfections arising from human frailty. The Son of God made all human conditions, except sin, his own when he became man. He was familiar with physical weariness after work and long wanderings and with spiritual and physical suffering. He was not even spared the agony of death. His humanity was no abstraction. By his language, culture, habits and probably even his features he was evidently typical of the Jewish people as they existed at that precise moment in history. It is the same with the Church and the only essential condition is that the human side should never overshadow or hide the divinity which is always her inspiration.

But nobody had thought of telling me that there is a Christian 'world' alongside the Church, as it were, and it took me years to become fully conscious of its complicated and deceptive reality. While I never regretted my conversion to the Church I must confess I found it very difficult to adapt myself to the conditions of this 'Christian world'—and the more I became absorbed in my religion the further away from that world I moved.

This 'Christian world' is the result of a more-or-less successful co-operation between the Church and given civilisations. As a rule the average Christian does not often distinguish between the convictions and reactions based on Christianity and those which come from the civilisation and society of which he is a member. He is in good faith when he attributes his actions to the dictates of a Christian conscience even though in actuality the motive force may be allegiance to his country or, on a lower plane, to his class.

A convert naturally cannot immediately distinguish between

the Christian 'world' and the Church and consequently makes an effort to adapt himself to circumstances. Some succeed very well, others not so well and I, for my part, never succeeded at all. I was astonished to find that not only is this 'world' in no way superior to any other world but that, precisely because of its claims to the high Christian ideals, its inadequacy is all the more blatant. The tragedy is that most people whom the Christian world fails blame the Church for their disappointment. It seems to me imperative that the Church make it clear that her status must not be confused with that of any worldly status, 'Christian' or otherwise. The material world came into being and in the course of time will disappear again but the Church holds the promise of duration until the end of time.

During certain epochs of its history the Church seems to have had such a strong influence on the lives of its members that their world could justly be called Christian. Gradually, and in proportion as western civilisation cut itself off from a sacramental life, the influence of the Church waned in a world which, by now, has almost ceased to believe and has practically forfeited all claims to be called Christian. It is tragic but inevitable that the Church herself cannot altogether escape the influence of this 'Christian world'.

Obviously the spiritual nature of the Church transcends all civilisations and boundaries be they geographical, social, cultural or psychological. But the Church is made up of men who, even though they speak in her name, cannot completely refrain from depending on and conforming with the world to which they belong both by ancestry and education. Although at times they sincerely believe in their struggle for the glory of God in reality they often fight merely for the survival of one particular society which at best is just one Christian society amongst many. A case in point is when the leaders or spokesmen of the Church make statements favouring one particular political regime, one form of ownership, one single philosophy or scientific concept.

A*

9

I hope that nobody will read into this an intention to vilify the Church of which I am a member and hope, by the grace of God, to remain a member until I die. I have no wish to act the part of prosecutor or inquisitor; neither Vishinsky nor Torquemada are heroes of mine. Nor am I the righteous man accusing others. I am merely a Christian who wonders about certain things and tries to reason them out.

The pages which follow are by no means the complete 'Diary of a Priest'—to think that would be to mistake a few trees for the whole forest. I find I have said very little about the truly deep joys that I experienced in the course of my life in the Church and that I have rarely mentioned the multitude of Christians I was fortunate enough to meet whose lives accord with the demands of the gospel. As the title indicates I have collected notes concerning the defects of the Christian society but I do not pretend for an instant that this society is wholly defective nor—let me emphasise it once more—is it identical with the Church.

I am well aware of the dangers of presenting this book to the public. Those who are in the habit of oversimplifying things and making hasty judgments might easily draw conclusions from it which by no means tally with my own. I hesitated a long time before publishing it but eventually decided to do so because many who had read *From Karl Marx to Jesus Christ* asked me to give an account of my experiences as a Christian. Many of the letters came from priests, religious and leaders of Catholic action. They maintained it would be a very good thing for the cradle Catholic to know how someone feels about them who shares their faith in our Lord but does not belong to their society. Catholics who read the manuscript reacted in the same way. But I think that if the conflicts and difficulties discussed in it had been purely personal ones I should probably have decided against publication. But I have had ample opportunity to see that many Christians, and many of them not converts, feel just as uneasy about the Christian society as I do. Many, both priests and laymen, who have always belonged to the Church are conscious of this society which, like a shadow, overcasts the radiance of the gospel.

One of my friends—an eminent Dominican theologian— to whom I showed the manuscript thought that my insistence on the 'rigorously sociological and phenomenological' aspect of Christianity was likely to be misunderstood by the general reader and that it was essential that Christianity be presented in a comprehensible form. The reverend father is quite right but the subject of this book dictated its form. One day I may be able to write a book which will show the eternal youth of the Church and the Holy Spirit's ever active presence in her— for miraculous as it may seem, in spite of the failure of Christians the Church continues to live in the undiminished strength of her ever-youthful vigour.

1941 — 2

15th July

I am in the train on my way to the south of France, to Marseilles, the town which providence has appointed as the first field of my priestly activities. God only knows what kind of work will be given me. I should like to devote myself to the welfare of the working classes to whom I owe so much and without whose help I should never have cracked the shell of my intellectual selfishness—nor ever come to be a priest. But what exactly do I know of their spiritual needs? Lately I have come to see that during my ten years' membership of the communist party I fought for the ideal man rather than for the real man. It seemed to me that human happiness could only be achieved on the terms laid down by Marx and Lenin and that, if the workers refused to conform to the party line and were crushed under the merciless heel of history, they had only themselves to blame.

The years in between, which I spent in preparing myself for the priesthood, taught me that every soul has an eternal value. However I must admit that neither today, nor at the time when I first came into contact with Christianity, has my primary concern ever been for the salvation of the individual soul. I am totally incapable of taking an interest in my own chances of heavenly bliss and probably shall never be able to promise a repentant sinner that his soul will be saved. The only thing which really matters to me is the *collective* destiny of mankind, or, rather, of the entire creation. Origen struggled with the same problem. He found it impossible to believe that on the day of the second coming of Christ, of the final completion of God's work, a single soul or being could be found wanting because if this were so we should have to admit that the redeeming act of Christ had failed. Yet this collectivity, this community, can only be an abstract idea unless it represents the sum total of all individual lives. So it seems that after all I shall have to take a special interest in every human being our Lord sends me.

27th July

Father A. under whose guidance I am serving my apprenticeship for the ministry, is remarkable both for his apostolic zeal and his piety. It is a pity I did not meet him years ago. A young colleague told me that he was a pioneer in the movement for the revival of parish life of the type I have so often admired in Lyons where practices such as Mass in the vernacular, Catholic action etc. have been introduced. Now, however, Father A. is squarely opposed to his enthusiams of those days; he is very much in favour of tradition in the liturgy and prefers to devote his time and energy to works of mercy, the Children of Mary and the Guild of the Blessed Sacrament, rather than to the furtherance of the Young Christian Workers which was formerly the object of his zeal. What surprises me more than anything else though is the unrelenting harshness with which he condemns modern philosophy and theology. None of my very esteemed teachers at the university in Lyons finds favour in his eyes. He even goes so far as to tell me that Henri de Lubac, author of *Catholicism* and the most intelligent and gracious man I have had the good fortune to meet, is little short of a dangerous heretic.

The morning after I arrived Father A. came to look at my books. The sight of the complete works of Bergson and Blondel worried him and since then he has not ceased warning me against the 'diabolical errors' of the two philosophers. Yet it was Bergson who first opened my eyes so that I began to wonder and gradually to become aware of the spiritual world while Blondel, it seems to me, has provided such an exhaustive synthesis of Christian thought and so solid a foundation for apologetics that it is bound to convince even the modern intellectual. What astonishes me, however, is that Father A. has never read either Bergson or Blondel and has only dipped

16

very slightly into Lubac's main work. But I am not so presumptuous as to think less of him for not being a philosopher; although for me there is no deeper joy than dealing with things of the mind I have learned to respect the man of action.

28th July

I have just learned the explanation of Father A.'s odd behaviour. During the war he was in the throes of a terrible moral dilemma and became attracted by a fairly enlightened Spanish priest, a former Jesuit, who had founded a retreat house somewhere in the country. There he converted many people by talking with great vigour about sin and hell and by pretending *to see the actual fire in hell.* He condemns everything modern both in the world and the Church. I was told that in this strange retreat house the famous anti-modernist encyclical *Syllabus* of Pius IX is accorded the same honour as the gospels and that this encyclical is used as authority for distrusting the writings of Teilhard de Chardin, Lubac, and Congar not to mention Bergson and Blondel. Even Maritain is suspect because he deemed it expedient to *adapt* Thomism to the mentality of the the twentieth century. As if there could be any doubt that the twentieth century is ruled by Satan!

This sort of thing is all new to me and I find it difficult to see my way. My dealings up to now have mainly been with Catholics who, far from censuring the modern world, have an admiration for its values and try to Christianise them. The teachers at the university of Lyons, the Jesuits of Fouvières, the Dominicans of Latour Maubourg; men like Mounier, Folliet, Maritain, organisations like the *Jeunesse d'Eglise, Espirit* and the *Thomas More Association* all of whom meet in Lyons; the men who are responsible for the *Chronique Sociale* whom I had the good fortune to meet—all these have more or less the same idea of Christianity and the part it is to play in the world. I remember being told about the 'Apostles of the Status Quo', the fanatical adherents to a Church policy of inflexible laws who detest the efforts for a revival of Christianity. Although up till a few days ago my knowledge of such people was purely theoretical I realise that suddenly I find myself in the middle of their camp!

3rd August

Mr R. the president of our parish union has just returned from a retreat at this retreat house and is greatly disturbed. He noticed that the men who took part (most of them either from curiosity or the desire to please their parish priest) were terribly upset by the passionate utterances of the preacher. But can anyone avoid feeling embarrassed when he is confronted with a certain form of showmanship such as, for instance, the talk on hell which was held in a darkened hall with a skull as the only thing visible? Yet this was not the first such retreat Mr R. had attended—he went there last year shortly after the death of Cardinal Verdier and he told me that during this famous and—it seems—particularly lively sermon on hell, the preacher suddenly raised his arms like a visionary and exclaimed 'I see him . . . I see him burning in hell'—and after a few minutes' silence—'I see the former Cardinal Verdier burning in hell'. It appears that in 1936 the then Archbishop incurred the father's displeasure because he was too sympathetic towards Blum's social policy and the government of the Popular Front. I find it difficult to believe this story but several other retreatants confirm it.

I am also told—and Father A. makes no secret of it—that the retreatant and his disciples lump together communists, socialists and Christian democrats all as 'reds' and thus candidates for damnation and hell fire!!

8th September

The other day a parishioner said to me 'Have you noticed that extraordinary girl Monette? She is studying medicine and she meditates half an hour every morning in Church before Mass, she pays a visit to the Blessed Sacrament every evening and in addition to that she is always trying to do good—she takes an active interest in the young girls of the parish and sees

18

to it that no one dies in hospital without having seen the priest.'

Now in fact I am somewhat awed to find so many virtues in one single person and I don't really know what imp of perversity prompts me to say: 'Yes, I have noticed Monette's piety and zeal and she only lacks one thing to be quite stupendous.'

'But she lacks nothing at all.'

'Oh yes, because in spite of her virtues and good works she has never yet had her head turned by a flighty young man and has never loved to distraction. If after experiencing her own frailty she returns to God then Monette will be truly marvellous.'

Have I been wise to scandalise this good lady, such a typical specimen of the average good Christian? I don't know, but I get so tired of these dear souls who only have a supercilious pity for the sinner. I am definitely more in sympathy with the latter.

30th September

A friend from Lyons has sent Clare to me, a Jewish girl who says she wants to become a Catholic. I have been instructing her for the past three days but all the time I couldn't help feeling she had a reason for wanting to be a Catholic that had nothing to do with religion. At last this afternoon she unburdened her heart and admitted that her real aim was to acquire a certificate of baptism, antedated by a few years, which would protect her from anti-Jewish persecution and possibly allow her to get a visa for one of the Latin-American countries. I explained that in these circumstances I could not receive her into the Church since in my view baptism was anything but a mere administrative formality. To my surprise my refusal wakened something in Clare's soul and, for the first time, she was all attention as I talked to her about our religion. Although I refused to receive her at the same time I promised to furnish her with the longed-for document. Why not? Surely a slight slip of the pen is justified when a human life is at stake?

25th October

Clare has been to see me again; in fact she has been here quite frequently although she has got her certificate and I even went to the consulate of one of the officially Catholic Latin American countries to get a visa for her. But now that she no longer has to concentrate on escaping danger she is really attracted to the religion of Jesus Christ. She is so eager to know about it that I can only marvel at the power of the Holy Ghost acting in her. Now it is my turn to urge her to be received into the Church as soon as possible so that she can take the ship which leaves next week. She would willingly miss it in order to prepare herself for the great mystery of union with Christ. So, if the bishop agrees, I shall baptise her tomorrow.

3rd December

This morning we celebrated a funeral mass and the Church was packed to capacity. Judging by the boredom on the people's faces most of them were not in the habit of attending Church and it was only the death of a relative, or a close friend, which had brought them there. I wonder whether we, the clergy, did all we could to make them conscious of the divine Presence and of the significance of the ceremony—or if they only saw it as a formality and a lot of hocus-pocus.

We sang the Mass and the Latin chant of the *Libera*, we incensed the coffin and sprinkled it with holy water. What did these men and women make of all those gestures and un-intelligible words?

This is not the first time I have been perturbed and puzzled by the atmosphere of mystery clinging to the ceremonies and liturgy of the Church. In St Albans in Lyons the priest used to give a clear and detailed explanation of the significance of each sacrament and refused to baptise a child unless its parents and its godparents agreed to undergo an introductory in-struction about the significance of the mystery. He also refused to bless a marriage unless he was convinced that it was really the sacrament and not a mere social formality he was expected to dispense. And he took great care that the engaged couple should really understand the sacredness of their future union.

Why don't we do this in every parish? A curate, a very devout young priest, told me the other day that he felt a sort of painful embarrassment every time he had to recite prayers in Latin in the presence of people who only entered a Church for a baptism, a wedding or a funeral. I know I shall be told that the sacraments work *ex opere operato* because Christ is present in them but if the expression is to be taken in that sense then I fail to see much difference between a sacramental ceremony and those magic rites of which the Church so much disapproves.

20th December

What is the best way to talk to children about God and our Lord in order that the catechism should really give them a living introduction to religion? I have watched catechism teachers, both priests and lay people, at work on various occasions. Some of them tell the story of the bible and the gospels exactly as one would tell a fairytale. Yet all these youngsters have long since ceased to believe in Father Christmas and Snow White and the rest. I can tell by the quizzical look on their faces that the stories about such events as the birth of Jesus, his miracles or tales of wonder from the Old Testament make no impression on them.

Other teachers follow the examples of some schools by trying to teach religion in the same way as biology, geography or history. That seems to go down better. It even surprises the children sometimes because many of them who come from the poorer quarters have had their religion presented to them, mainly by their grandmothers, as a series of fabulous events. On the other hand they *are* children and I have heard them clamouring for the 'story of the apple' when the teacher was speaking about original sin and explaining that it results in our disobedience to God's commandments. This 'scientific' approach certainly results in the children *knowing* their doctrine

—but how are we to impart the faith, how can we touch the hearts of these young creatures? This problem seems to me terribly pressing because sooner or later when the children go to a secular school Catholic doctrine will be challenged by other doctrines—and what incentive will these children have to believe in the truth of the Catholic ones?

I went to see some friends the other day and their nine-year-old son who is just learning his catechism gave me a very searching look and said: 'Surely *you* don't believe all the silly things Father X is telling us?'

1942

20th January

Yesterday I ran into J. He and I were received into the Church at about the same time and we always felt drawn to each other. He used to be a lawyer and after his conversion became a Dominican. As he did not believe that God had called him from so far off and had helped him to overcome so many obstacles just for the sake of solving the scrupulosities of the dear old ladies of the Third Order, and moreover knowing from experience just how little notice the modern world takes of God (a state of which few cradle Catholics are really aware) he decided he must try to take our Lord back into the world.

His charity induced him to join hands with the very poor and he became a docker at Marseilles. At first he had no idea what he ought to do—the one thing that mattered was that Christ, in his priest, should work and live among the most despised of his sons. For many months his fellow workers did not know that he was a priest.

If our Lord came back to live in the world today I hardly think he would be a craftsman in a little village but more probably a factory worker—or a Marseilles docker. Anyone who reads the gospel carefully and without prejudice cannot fail to see how outrageously the poor of that day were exploited by the wealthy; the justice Christ would preach today would be first and foremost what we nowadays call social justice. So J. took the line he thought his Master would most probably take.

Before long J. was in the forefront of the dockers' battle for better pay and more social recognition. They were astonished when one day he had to reveal his priesthood—they had been quite determined that he should marry and many of them had set their heart on welcoming him into their own family. To think that a priest could be such a good sort and really one of themselves! The yard manager, himself a Catholic, was no less surprised but not nearly so pleased. He could have understood and even approved of a priest becoming a worker in order to 'convert' his fellow workers and preach Christian meekness as an antidote to communism. But how disgraceful and what a betrayal of holy orders for a priest—and a well educated one at that—to join the ranks of the agitators and be a radical himself!

J. told me this and much else besides with his usual indulgent smile. He did not criticise the manager because he understood how he felt—but that did not deter him from persevering in his fight.

25th February

I have just been reading the *Apologia* of Cardinal Newman to whom the Catholic revival in Anglo-Saxon countries owes so much. The title rather shocked me—against whom did a man like Newman, who lived a good life and was admired by his former parishioners for his piety, have to defend himself?— Could his former co-religionists not forgive him for deserting the Church of England or did the atheists hate and attack him? Alas no, Newman found that, far from killing the fatted calf to celebrate the return to the fold of a lost sheep—much less being grateful that the Lord had brought such a truly great man into the Church—the Catholics proceeded to calumniate and persecute him. They suspected his motives and created such an atmosphere of suspicion and ill will round him that it could hardly fail to wound his extremely sensitive nature. It was almost as if they had a grievance against God for having converted him—even provided they admitted it *was* God who had called him!

It reminds me of another convert I met some years ago. He had been a leading figure among Dutch Protestants and a Minister of Education. He then became a Catholic although doing so meant breaking many good friendships and giving up his office. But don't imagine for a moment that the Catholics were quick to welcome him—nothing of the sort. Although some of them were pleased about his conversion apparently that was because it confounded their religious rivals. Few took the trouble to understand his motives and most criticised his behaviour whenever it did not conform to that of cradle Catholics. Any convert had better think twice before he criticises Catholics and their way of clinging to mere habits. He must admire the pious pictures in their homes and the awful plaster statues in many of the churches and it goes without saying that in future he must vote only for the Catholic party. As if the Church of Christ could be identified with one particular political party, one style or one special branch of philosophy.

26th February

At the time when I spoke to the Dutch convert and he told me of the difficulties he had to find his feet in the world of Catholics I did not quite know what to make of it. I had only recently joined the Church myself and had not had a parallel experience. The leftist Catholics, both priests and laity, among whom I lived up to the time of my ordination had never made me feel I was a stranger. Their charity, which I was quite unconscious of at the time but which I fully appreciate today, made them bear with my sometimes very odd behaviour.

Reading the *Apologia* and remembering what the Dutchman had said suddenly brought home to me the ambiguous position I occupy in the Christian 'world'—which is not to be confused

24

with the Church. When I first came into contact with the general Christian society I did so as a priest and as such in a fortunate position. I made no secret of being a convert and a former communist, nor was it resented; indeed people even congratulated me on having realised my error and discovered the truth. This apparent generosity encouraged me and I felt it to be my duty to preach Christ's message as it had captivated me and as I understand it. That is where I went wrong.

The Catholic 'world' is prepared to accept me on condition that I am grateful for the honour they do me by making me welcome. I had become a Christian as soon as I realised that the truth to which I had formerly adhered was to be found in the dogma of the Church. It seems that the fact of my believing in the triune God, the Incarnation, the Redemption and the real Presence in the eucharist is accepted as a matter of course but the Christian society is beginning to wonder about my belief in 'Christian values'.

The other evening I was invited to a dinner party at the house of a Catholic prominent in the town's social life. Naturally the conversation turned to my communist past and I had to answer questions about Russia and my reasons for leaving it and breaking with the party. Perhaps I could not sufficiently portray the type of man I was at the time of my break with the communists for my words to have any impact on the assembled guests. At any rate I was perfectly sincere in what I said and I tried to explain to these good Catholics that I disapproved of communism because of its materialism, its contempt for the individual and the practical consequences of that contempt, as well as its systematic negation of all spiritual values. The guests listened patiently but I couldn't help noticing they were only mildly interested and soon the conversation turned to 'serious matters' such as the blow communism has dealt to the sacrosanct right of private property, the violation of the truth that 'men are not all born equal' and the denial of the creed that 'only free enterprise is in favour of private initiative and thus of human progress' and the rest of the usual grievances the middle class cherish against communism.

It would probably have been wiser to keep quiet and say nothing but this is not the first time my evil genius has led me to say the right thing at the wrong moment. So I told my listeners how terribly disappointed I was when I realised that Stalin had dissociated himself from the egalitarian ideal of socialism and that, as a result, the old social differences between individuals had become noticeable again in Russia and a gulf opened between the various social categories.

I don't really know whether my words caused more scepticism or more scandal but at any rate it was obvious that nobody accepted a word of what I had said. I couldn't help wondering if these good Christians would have been quite so anti-Communist—in spite of its atheist materialism and its hatred of spiritual values—if they *had* believed what I told them about the new trend in Russia. And when, to prove my case, I compared the religious persecutions and the rigged trials in the U.S.S.R. with the Jewish persecutions and the death camps of the Nazi regime I was told 'But that is something entirely different'. Where is the difference? Is it possible that these 'good Catholics' are somehow, under the surface, in sympathy with Hitler as long as he expresses anti-capitalism only in words and not in action?

As for my own reputation I could see in their faces and their attitude to me that from now onwards I am labelled as Utopian. My host in his gentle way even put it into words when he said 'After all it is such a short time since you became a Christian that it is no wonder you have not been able to rid yourself entirely of the Marxist poison'.

1st August

I have been appointed to act as chaplain to a camp of girl students and so, a few days ago, I came to this place in the mountains near Chamonix and the Swiss border at the foot of Mont le Buet. It is one of the most marvellous spots I have ever come across. Every morning while I wait for the girls to get ready I walk up the path saying my Office and whenever I look up there are snow covered peaks of Mont Blanc and the others. Never till now have I realised how much the splendours of nature help the soul and further its ascent towards God. In church I often feel oppressed by the numerous ugly statues and paintings and the conventional postures of the religious bigots at their devotions. Here it is quite different and I don't wonder that the young people are so absorbed in their prayers when Mass is said on top of a mountain.

It seems a pity we can't do this every day but the Church authorities have laid down certain rules for holiday camps by which we chaplains must abide at least in broad outline. So it is in a shed that I usually celebrate the holy sacrifice of the Mass. That is all right because with a little good will it can remind us of the stable in Bethlehem. But our 'confessional' is absolutely ludicrous. The regulation states that in the confessional women must be separated by a grille from their confessor but as it is difficult to come by a grille in this place, the camp leader, a devout girl, a medical student from Grenoble who happens to have a sense of humour, has solved the problem (at least technically) by suspending from the ceiling a large saucepan lid! But I can't help wondering what some of the students who are here in contact with a priest for the first time in years, make of a religion which, according to the spirit of its Founder, ought not to be restricted by formalities but should be free to live *in the spirit and in truth*.

3rd August

Helen, the camp leader, has just warned me that some of the girls who are full of the spirit of the 'national revolution' are disgusted with me and my careless way of standing to attention during the 'salute to the flag'. Incidentally the whole camp assembles morning and evening round the flag and sings 'Maréchal, nous voila'. I am accused of standing lost in thought instead of at attention; but although I can truthfully say that until this morning I did it quite unconsciously because I am not military minded and the cult of the 'Marshall' means nothing to me whatsoever, I admit that in future I shall do it on purpose.

5th August

A minor revolution has broken out in the camp next to ours. The chaplain, a young Dominican, roused the students' indignation by giving the impression that he did not take them very seriously. In the eyes of women anywhere but most particularly young intellectual women he couldn't have committed a worse crime. It was certainly not very clever of him to ignore this most elementary rule of the psychology of women, or for that matter, psychology as such. His recent studies have taught him that the solution of every problem past, present or future can be found in St Thomas's *Summa* and he is never without a pocket edition. Whenever a student submits an intellectual or a moral problem he pulls out the *Summa* and proceeds, with visible pleasure, to prove that St Thomas anticipated the question and provided the answer. Then of course he is free to quote from the text as he pleases.

I am not surprised the girls revolted. Most of us are convinced that we are unique and have to face new and quite unheard-of conflicts of conscience. And young people, particularly young women, feel this very strongly. The girls wanted the priest to listen to their personal problems, take the trouble to understand their inner feelings and suggest solutions adapted to their very particular case. The Dominican's ready-made and seven-hundred-years-old answers are obviously quite inadequate for present day needs. For my part I don't think the girls are entirely wrong; if the Father consults me I shall try to suggest he might do better to leave the book in his cell and be all the better prepared to be inspired by his beloved master.

8th August

We had an interesting meeting of ten chaplains and ten camp leaders. The latter are usually students in their final year and Young Christian Workers with a certain amount of experience. What I like about them is that they speak their minds openly to each other as well as to the priests. I believe that for some among us priests it is the first time that lay people have told us what they really think of us; I am sure that even though today, thanks to Catholic Action, the priests are in closer contact with the laity, false respect for the priesthood still prevents people being frank—and possibly brutal—with us and they thus fail to provide us with something we badly need—a true picture of ourselves.

After discussing the details necessary for the smooth running of the organisation of these ten camps we tackled the problem of the relations between the students and their chaplains. We, the chaplains, are accused of being either too familiar or too distant. It seems that some of us aim so high in our talks that we are far above the students' heads and they get no benefit at all, while others are so childish in their approach that it gives a very poor idea of the Christian message and its intellectual potentialities to an audience accustomed to the standards of university lecturers.

Finally the chief chaplain asked the camp leaders to tell us quite honestly what particular qualities the girls look for in their chaplains. They mentioned among other things intelligence, perception, sensitivity etc. but most of us chaplains were surprised to hear the leaders unanimously require that a priest should above all be a *man*—a 'real male' as some of them put it. It seems the girls don't like effeminate types, the shy and reserved priest who, they claim, isn't able to advise on the 'real problems of life'.

After having attended innumerable boring gatherings in Marseilles of Catholics of the various movements and charitable groups I find it very exhilarating to be among these camp leaders. But I wonder whether their Christian way of thinking is not in part at least due to the purifying air of this high mountain and whether they will become dull and formal

29

like most of the others as soon as they return to their homes.

9th August

Helen asked me to change my place in the dining hall as, although I hadn't noticed, the same girl always sat on my right; such things, she said, make for jealousy. It seems that not everybody is purified by the heights!

15th August

I left the camp the better for a marvellous experience. Now I am convinced that if there is a personal mission for me in the Church of God it can only be in the intellectual sphere. It was only after an inner struggle that I accepted this fact because at heart I am much more in sympathy with simple poor people, particularly those among the proletariat who belong to that class and know it. When I am in the company of well-to-do Christians I am never able to feel such a deep sense of communion as I do amongst the YCW or the Popular Family movement. But I have to admit that I am incapable of giving them what I would so dearly love to give them and what they have a right to expect from me. Whether I like it or not I am an intellectual. With people who are at home in the world of thought I am immediately in contact and find the way to their heart and spirit without any trouble whereas with the workers I am awkward and hardly ever able to hit the right note.

Later, in Chambery

I broke my journey to go to see someone I had corresponded with and on leaving the house I saw a distinguished looking priest with the insignia of a canon. I asked him the way to the cathedral and he told me that he was the resident priest and offered to take me there and as we walked I told him where I had been and where I was going and when he had shown me the cathedral he took me back to his house, insisted on my sharing his meal and finally went with me to the station. I was deeply touched by this instance of true priestly brotherhood because I have only rarely come across it. At the

30

beginning of my priestly career I imagined that the ties between priests were at least as close as those between militant communists but I was disillusioned only too soon. It is true that, outside Paris, priests raise their hats to each other when they meet in the street but it is only a gesture of reverence to the religious garb. Usually each of them remains in his own ivory tower with no interest in his 'dear brethren' except when one of them is suspected of having trespassed against the ecclesiastical conventions. So my gratitude goes out to that priest in Chambery for having shown me quite another aspect of priestly fraternity.

18th August

When I got back from the camp a librarian in Marseilles invited me to spend a few days in the High Alps at the castle of St Leger. I don't mean that he owns the castle for in fact no one knows who really does own the dilapidated pile. But it is a rest centre for all Christians who feel out of place in the individualistic and at the same time impersonal atmosphere of the usual parish. The driving force behind this venture is an innkeeper from Gap and every summer men and women from all stations of life meet at St Leger to discuss their problems— lecturers, teachers, business men, labourers, engineers, students, doctors, lawyers and artists. We spent our time in praying the liturgy (in the vernacular), studying, and having walks and discussions and we also peeled potatoes, chopped wood and carried water. It was all very simple and unsophisticated and judging from the peace and joy on the faces of the visitors they seemed to have forgotten the upheavals of their daily lives. In this place Christian brotherhood is no mere slogan but concrete reality lived day by day and I wonder how many religious houses there are where the charity of Christ is practised so genuinely. What a tragedy that this communal life is restricted to a few weeks in the year and that I can only stay a few days. But on the other hand perhaps it is as well because if these men and women lived all the time in this community they would probably be even less able than a religious community to avoid the effects of routine and the small pinpricks of daily life. In its present form the communal life in St Leger seems to supply its guests with the renewal of energy they need if they are not to be crushed under the weight of the fearful pharasaical conventionalism of most of our parishes. I personally came away with a profound sense of joy and peace.

15th October

I have never resigned myself to Nazi victory and in Lyons I worked with men and women who wrote and distributed de Gaullist literature. Later I joined up with the editors of *Témoinage Chrétien* but it was not until last night that I was officially brought into contact with the underground movement. A friend from Nimes sent me a rather cryptic letter announcing the visit of a friend who 'deserved our full confidence'. He came and asked me to put him in touch with young men of courage and discretion. Then to my surprise he produced from his brief case a parcel of identity cards, ration cards, police stamps and so on. He explained what it was all for and I must confess it wasn't without anxiety that I agreed to look after this all-too-compromising material. I am no more immune to search than anyone else and I have already been in so many prisons that I have no desire at all to enlarge my experience in this field. But since my heart and my head both tell me I must make common cause with the resistance I have certainly no right to refuse when they expect me to share the risks they run.

16th October

Alas I am definitely not of the stuff conspirators are made of. Since I have agreed to join the underground I really ought to refrain from telling everybody what I think of the Nazis and the Vichy collaborators. Yet I can't stop myself and it is quite impossible for me to keep silent when I hear people praising Pétain and repeating the slogans about a new Europe and antibolshevist crusade to which Radio Vichy and Radio Paris

32

treat them day in and day out—and I absolutely seethe with rage if I hear priests talking like this. I have just had a violent argument about it with two of my 'brethren' and they have threatened to lodge a complaint against me—not with the police but with the bishop! His Lordship is not pro-Nazi because he is too much a man of the Church but he is the son of a wealthy industrialist and is essentially a man for order. I have had several occasions of discussing this subject with him and once when I told him that I personally preferred the rather haphazard methods of democracies to the so-called authoritarian regimes he quoted 'The worst order is better than the best disorder'. So naturally he is in favour of the Vichy government, particularly as he hopes that Pétain will establish *moral* order in France. Some hope. But obviously I am not the right person to persuade him that he is wrong. But at least I know that he would never, as did the archbishop of a nearby diocese, take disciplinary action against priests denounced to him as de Gaullists.

20th October

Emmanuel Mounier has been in prison now for some time. In 1940 when Pétain ousted Laval, Mounier was foolish enough to believe that law and order could be established under the 'National Revolution' regime and gave his permission for the journal *Esprit* to reappear in Lyons. He very soon realised that he couldn't continue unless he was prepared to betray what the review and its director had always held to be the truth—and in fact the government suppressed the review. But the secret police were bound to notice the influence he exercised in the intellectual circles of Lyons and indeed in the entire unoccupied zone. Although they never found any incriminating material (not for want of trying) they imprisoned him and kept him in prison even though after months no evidence could be produced against him. It seems incredible but it is nevertheless true that the wholly illegal regime is very anxious to preserve an appearance of justice.

A friend of mine told me of the long hunger strike which Mounier has imposed on himself in prison. A few days ago he felt his strength fading and fearing to die almost at once he asked for a priest so that he could receive absolution and Holy Communion. But the priest (I shouldn't be surprised to hear that he was a 'holy man') refused him absolution on the grounds that he had disobeyed legitimate authority and was not prepared to repent his disobedience. There seems no limit to the stupidity of men, even of priests. One sometimes needs great strength and pure faith not to be discouraged and to remain loyal to the Church almost, as it were, in spite of herself.

1st December

Last night I had a heated discussion with a few fellow priests on the subject of the publication of the underground paper *Témoinage Chrétien*. They cannot understand why Catholics in public life and priests should edit this paper and it was no use my trying to point out that the Vichy government is not a divine institution. In the eyes of these well-meaning priests it is only communists, enemies both of God and of France, who are interested in sabotaging the efforts of the 'national revolution' which this government claims as its own. At this moment when the allied landing in North Africa gives us more reason to doubt the final victory of the Nazis these good priests are still utterly convinced of it.

It is not that they *want* German victory because not one of them upholds Nazi-ism but the training they received at the seminaries has formed their intellect on such exclusively abstract lines that they are unable to cope with practical life and they battle against dilemmas which exist only in their minds. Listening to them one would imagine that France and the world must choose either Hitler or Stalin—or, in other words, between a 'New Europe' under Nazi leadership or the occupation of Europe by the 'red hordes'. Whatever the Nazi crimes, to these priests they seem less terrifying than the horrors for which the communists are responsible. It is quite impossible to convince them that there is a possibility of avoiding the domination of both Hitler and Stalin. And if one mentions the possible return of a French parliamentary democracy they repeat all the Vichy banalities about the corruption and decadence of the 'people's republic' with a fervour worthy of a better cause.

This state of affairs makes me reflect on the collective psychological complexes which account for the favourable disposition of the Catholic world in general with regard to this 'national revolution'. Of course there are always opportunists ready to support the winning side but in general they are less numerous among Catholics than other bodies. There are also people who have been influenced by the writings of Maurras and who naturally rejoice to see the end of an atheistic trend. But both these represent only a small minority among Catholics and are practically non-existent among the young clergy. So that it does seem that when most of my co-religionists— with the exception of some young clergy influenced by Catholic Action training—acclaimed the 'national revolution' they were certainly not doing so from selfish motives.

It shocks me to think of all the Catholics who made no protest when some of their preachers had no scruples in flattering Pétain and acclaiming him as a sort of Joan of Arc. Even Péguy, the typical individualist, finds he is called upon to comply with the worst kind of pseudo-Christian principles. Pétain is known to be no more religious minded than Paul Reynaud and yet all sorts of legends are invented to make him out a sort of saint. His entourage are shrewd enough to encourage these legends because they realise that numerically the Catholics are the only class on which the regime could stand. It seems as if the nostalgia for a theocratic regime is still prevalent among Catholics—how otherwise can one explain why the confusion between religious and political views is so welcome to them. Not only have the subsidies for denominational schools been welcomed with real gratitude but many people hope and trust that Pétain will restore the establishment of the Church in France.

The authoritarian character of the Church has developed in many Catholics a tendency to evade all spiritual responsibility; they assert that the Church is the steward of eternal truth and then content themselves with repeating mechanically the liturgical and dogmatic formulas without making an intelligent effort to understand them and bring them to life. They seem to have lost the determination to obey moral laws; all they are concerned with is to be told by authority what to do and what not to do. I find it hard to believe that this is what Christ came for but, as far as the subconscious mind of many Catholics is concerned, a long time has elapsed since evangelical liberty was supplanted by pharisaical observance of the law. So it is not surprising that these Catholics also tend to evade the personal responsibilities in the sphere of temporal organisations. If a democracy is not to deteriorate into a mere demagogy each person must be prepared to look after his own affairs and to contribute to the affairs of the community. It is so much easier to leave it all trustingly to the leader—Franco in Spain, Pétain in France; even the atheists Mussolini and Hitler know how to make the most of this inertia. Our Lord had good reason to speak of 'sheep' when he charged Peter to take care of his Church.

16th December

Miss A., a pious lady in her fifties, who devotes much of her time to parish work came to tell me with great indignation about her recent experience in the confessional. The conversation went like this:

Miss A.: Father, I have had sinful thoughts.

Priest: What type of thoughts?

Miss A.: Well, Father, impure thoughts, of course.

Priest (turning a deaf ear): Do you mean you have failed in the love of your neighbour?

Miss A.: No I don't. I have had evil thoughts.

> Priest: Do you mean that you had evil thoughts with
> regard to your brethren?

And so, Miss A. told me, the dialogue went on for some time. I explained that the priest was trying to make her understand that the Christian religion does not only consist in scrupulously observing the laws of chastity and that it is eminently important to spread the light of love with which God has entrusted us. It was sheer waste of time though she did admit that on Saturday evenings after confession she went to the bridge table and spent a good few hours there playing cards and running down her neighbours, beginning with the priest. And then on Sunday morning, her conscience in no way troubled, and like one justified, she kneels by the communion rail and receives our Lord. If, on the other hand, in the early morning before she is fully conscious a fleeting sexual desire passes through her mind she would feel she ought to go to confession before receiving Holy Communion.

We come up so frequently against these distorted ideas that I think we ought to expose them. While obviously I don't mean to minimise the gravity of carnal sin, it is equally certain that Christianity is not merely a sexual moral code. I think it may be because people are too often taken to task over this sin, particularly in the confessional, that one finds the obsession with regard to sex more frequently among pious people than among others. A few days ago I tried to persuade a woman it was wrong to accuse herself in confession of 'having found pleasure in the fulfilment of her marital duties'. She seemed disgusted with me when I told her that she not only had a right to this pleasure but that it formed an integral part of her marital duties. Many people seem to think that a duty must necessarily be irksome. I mentioned this point to a priest who is a very experienced director of souls and he told me that this type of idea was rare nowadays whereas some years ago it was a daily occurrence.

37

1943 — 4

9th January

Why is it permitted—why do we, the priests, permit—that the dealers sully the temple of God? We read in the gospel that our Lord made a scourge and drove the money changers and the dealers from his Father's house. Do priests no longer read the gospel or has it become such a habit that its revolutionary power no longer grips us? Devout women have stalls in nearly every church in Marseilles where they offer newspapers, holy pictures and rosaries for sale. Some of the profit goes to the priest yet neither he nor the poor woman are any better off for it. As for the apostolic value of such trade one need only watch the faces and listen to the comments of the passers-by. Notre Dame de la Garde on days of pilgrimage is more like a fair than anything else.

Except for a few priests in middle class parishes who have an occasional 'windfall' most priests in Marseilles and the south of France are poor, many of them very poor. I know quite a number who are literally hungry and it is not because they are miserly that their cassocks are green with age; while as for their shirts the vergers would scorn to be seen in them.

Such poverty is nothing to be ashamed of. I have known militant communists who have gladly accepted poverty and prison to be of better service to the party so I see no reason why the priests of Christ should not do the same—and in fact very rarely do any of them complain. The great majority accept poverty, if not with joy, at least with indifference. Money matters are last on the list of things discussed at clergy meetings and I cannot remember a single instance of a priest demanding better living conditions. The continuous clink of coins near the altar is therefore all the more offensive. During the first months of my priesthood I had the greatest difficulty in concentrating while celebrating Sunday Mass because I was so distracted by the incessant chink of coins. The plate was passed the first time almost as soon as Mass had begun and again after the sermon and this time it was the parish priest himself who, with a sacristan or a choir boy, collected for the repose of the holy souls. Sometimes there was a third collection after Communion for some special purpose and at the end of Mass the Legionaries or the Society of S. Vincent de Paul or the scouts or the Children of Mary waited by the door to receive contributions for their respective organisations.

Now all these collections bring in very little money—in fact quite ridiculously little—but they do a great deal of harm to the reputation of the Church and its ministers because they create a money complex whenever the Church is mentioned. At the beginning of Mass the father of each family distributes coins among their children so that each child can put something in each plate. They would feel embarrassed if they had to let one plate pass by even if they had put a bank note in the first one. While most of the priests take very good care not to look how much each person gives the sacristans have been known to look daggers at anyone letting the plate pass. And one result of all this is that the poorest priests have the irksome reputation of being well off. They rarely talk about their financial position, partly out of a sense of false modesty, partly from fear of middle-class prejudice.

Non-practising Catholics more than any others associate the image of a priest with that of a man holding out his hand—not to grasp the other man's hand in friendship but to catch hold of the collection. Such people usually only enter a church for a christening, a wedding or funeral or their child's first Communion and on these occasions the taking of collections is very prominent; on occasions they are organised with a naive ingenuity—as at one wedding where the bridesmaids were asked to pass the plate round. In some parishes, particularly if there is only one priest, Mass is interrupted before the Credo so that the priest himself can take the collection lest the congregation be less generous than they might be if the task were entrusted to voluntary helpers. A favourite story with young curates is that of the priest who announced 'the solemn collection during which High Mass would be taken'. But they can't see how terrible a story it is.

Father X, a fervent young curate, told me he recently went to visit a little girl who had been ill and away from the catechism class. Her parents rarely go to church and no sooner had her mother opened the door than, seeing him standing there, without even greeting him she called to her husband 'Jim here's Father X to collect for the church'. It took him some time to explain that he had not come for that purpose at all but had other, more important, reasons for looking them up. When he left he couldn't avoid having an envelope slipped in his hand—'For your trouble', they said, using the euphemism current among people who want to give money to the priest.

Can we not change these customs? Some parishes are trying. They have dispensed with collections; people who only come to church occasionally are never asked to contribute and the priests leave the care for their material needs in the hands of the practising Catholics. And the faithful are kept informed about the parish's financial affairs. The method seems to yield excellent results, particularly in those parishes where the priests have taken the trouble to train their flock so that they consider the church to be as much their affair as the parish priest's.

Yesterday I discussed this same problem with a very old-fashioned priest. He made no demur when I remarked how disgraceful I thought the interminable collections and how much harm I thought they did to the reputation of the Church. He was not afraid that if he left the care of parochial money matters to the laity he would receive less material help. But he was absolutely adamant that he would not let the laity, even the most trustworthy among them, know to what use the contributions were put. It suddenly dawned on me that it is far more the clericalism of the priests, rather than greed for money, which is behind some of the attitudes they adopt.

3rd March

Seven young men and women—students at the local training college for teachers—came to see me today. They have all been active YCS members for some time and it has made them conscious of the exacting demands of a truly evangelical Christianity. And they have begun to discover how difficult—almost impossible—it is to be in and of the modern world and yet live a truly Christian life. Their families are Catholic but mostly only nominally. The YCS demands that they inspire their charges but where are they themselves to find the spiritual food they so badly need. Our discussion went on for hours. I am hardly so presumptuous as to imagine that I can give them the spiritual nourishment they cannot find in their families or in their parishes. But have I any right to disappoint them and tell them their case is hopeless? We decided to meet again here in a week's time when they will bring some of their friends.

10th March

Today fifteen young people came to the first meeting of our 'community', the YCS leaders being accompanied by scout and guide captains who all labour under the same difficulties. We have no intention of forming yet another 'movement' and we certainly don't want to compete in any way with existing ones—in fact to make this point quite clear to ourselves we agreed that each present and future member of the 'community' must also belong to one or other of the action groups.

Since our first meeting last week the original seven had been to a lecture by Paul Reuter, Professor of Law at Aix, who had spoken of the dangers and temptations with which Nazism threatens mankind in general and Christianity in particular. He said he would not be surprised to see large scale religious persecution but if that did not develop the danger of a compromise with anti-Christian teaching would be at least as great. And he stressed how difficult it is for a solitary Christian to hold out against both the persecutors and the tempting promises of the false prophets and how imperative it is that Christians should band together in small communities. This really confirmed our decision to set up as a *community*. We shall have neither president nor secretary and instead of being chaplain I am simply a priest member putting the resources of my priesthood at the disposal of the community.

Now as reasoning creatures we can hardly claim to be Christians if we do not make the fullest possible use of our reason in Christ's service. So we have decided that one of the community's main objects will be the careful study of the various problems of existence. We are not concerned with speculating on possible theoretical solutions or with running a study circle at a higher intellectual level than usual. Our aim is to find solutions to the real problems in the life of the muni-cipality, the family and each of us individually, by assessing them in the light of Christian teaching. But we also want to contribute to the 'community' more than our small—or large as the case may be—intellectual gifts; it was suggested that we should pay our money into a common purse but it is not practicable, at least for the time being, since most of us depend entirely on allowances from our families.

In the meantime and until such time as the Holy Ghost shall choose to point the way, we shall try to live as near as possible to each other, to pray together as often as possible, share our ambitions and ideas and be united, as much as possible, in a spirit of brotherhood.

11th March

I have been told of a retired Colonel in Marseilles, a con-scientious and devout man, a Dominican tertiary and member of various religious organisations who has a peculiar twist that leads him to specialise in collecting indulgences. He pursues his hobby with the same fanatical devotion as collectors of stamps, paintings, butterflies and the rest. Each evening he records in a large account book every indulgence gained during the day, its kind and the number of days of 'sins remitted'. At the bottom of the page he adds up the days, months and years and carries them forward to the next page. Unfortunately he recently showed his account book to one of the Dominican fathers who, believing in shock tactics, flung the book in the fire. The Colonel was both nonplussed and deeply hurt.

This case of bigotry gave me a better insight into Luther's reasons for campaigning against the traffic in indulgences than any history of the reformation has ever done. And I also realised how grateful we ought to be that in the modern world indulgences can no longer be used as a source of income. I am fully aware of the theological explanation of the doctrine but after this affair somehow I am not too keen about gaining indulgences. May our Lord himself assess the value of my inadequate prayers and use them as he sees fit.

25th March

Austin, son of a rich and devout Catholic business man, told me that as he was coming out of the house he met his father who asked him where he was going. When he said he was on his way to see me his father replied 'Listen to anything he has to say about God and our Lady but if he starts talking about this world's affairs turn a deaf ear'. So now I know for certain that Marseilles 'society' regards me as a dangerous revolutionary although because of Vichy and gestapo spies I have forced myself to be extremely careful whenever I have given an opinion on political or social matters. The only place I mention these things is the school for social workers where I lecture on sociology and even then I always refer them to the papal encyclicals when I deal with social justice and its claims, or have to explain the advantages of democracy compared with other forms of government. But I know I am very undiplomatic and quite incapable of hiding my feelings.

As for Austin's father he and I had a few very polite discussions when I tried to make him see that doing good was not

46

sufficient and that so much depended on why and how it was done. He is very proud of his social achievements among his workers but he cannot admit that rather than remain the driving force himself and charge others with carrying out his improvements, he would do better to entrust the workers with the management of their own affairs. He is determined to be boss and to remain boss in the full sense of the word.

But I am accused of being 'revolutionary' not so much on account of my 'advanced' ideas on wages and co-partnership in industry but because I spoke in favour of a marriage between a young girl, daughter of a very old-established upper middle class family and a boy who, intellectually brilliant and of fine character, happens to be the son of a minor government worker. During one very fashionable dinner party I am told, it was seriously debated whether I was not really an agent of the communist party who had been parachuted into the Church for the purpose of laying the axe to the roots of the 'Christian family'.

It reminds me of a story told me by an old priest in Lyons, himself a member of a very wealthy family. One of his cousins had married a girl who, like himself, was a fervent and active Christian and they both tried to lead a truly Christian married life as the Church understands and interprets it. But the young man's family refused to receive the couple in their houses because, so they claimed, this *mesalliance* gravely imperilled the sacrosanct principles of the 'Christian family', however Christian the marriage appeared to be. But—and this is the real point—the eldest son and his wife, who were known to have little or no use for religion and to go their own sweet way, were very welcome at the parental mansion because *he* had married a girl of his own class. The worst of it is that these Christians, who undoubtedly take their religion seriously, are apparently quite unaware that they perpetually add to the confusion between true Christian morals and mere class prejudices.

3rd May

The parish priest of one of the most elegant quarters of the town has introduced a new practice during Mass which he is trying to enforce. He tells his congregation that as Christ himself taught his disciples to pray the *Our Father*, as a symbolic act of Christian brotherhood he expects the people to hold their neighbours' hands while the prayer is being prayed. This would seem a reasonable sort of demand but nevertheless in spite of the respect his people have for him he finds it very difficult to get them to comply. Most of them timidly brush their neighbours' finger tips and leave it at that. It is at least debatable whether even this gesture is made in a spirit of good-will.

The trouble is that in general each person assists at Mass either for himself or for the people to whom he feels naturally drawn and while the sermon, according to custom begins with the words 'My dear brethren in Jesus Christ' the wealthy merchant in the third row does not appear to consider his neighbour, who may be his charwoman, to be his sister. It looks as if the five hundred odd people who assemble at Mass meet there purely by chance and the more I see of this the more I realise the gulf between the present day parish and the Christian communities of the first centuries. Individualism, which has caused a great deal of harm to temporal society, has also, with more dangerous results, penetrated into the sheep-fold which our Lord entrusted to Peter.

During my life as an active communist I used to experience the almost magical power of the word 'comrade'; it was by using this term that we professed our joint allegiance to the great army of the revolution. When I became a member of the Church I believed for some years that the feeling of Christian brotherhood must needs be infinitely more apparent because Christians, as children of the heavenly Father, would necessarily be very dear to one another. Alas ...!

20th June

After a few months' existence the pattern of our little

48

'community' is beginning to emerge. It is quite evident that we are united by stronger bonds than those which exist between good friends, fellow-workers or even a band of activitists. The other day we invited Father Y. to be the guest at our weekly family meal and he told me afterwards that he distinctly felt the presence of a communal spirit—the manifest effect of the divine Spirit resting on every member and above all on the assembly.

Yet we have done nothing extraordinary. We meet one evening a week, usually at my place, and every member brings some food which is pooled and then we eat and chat. After the meal the member chosen the previous week gives a talk on the problem which to our minds needs special study and this is followed by a discussion during which some have much to say and others hardly open their mouths. But all the same everybody joins in the effort of trying to find a solution. Before we break up we recite Compline. Every Saturday morning they assist at my Mass and afterwards we breakfast together.

It seems to me that our joint excursions are largely responsible for the prevailing spirit of 'communion'. Sometimes we leave Marseilles on Saturday evening, spend the night at the country house of one of the members and get up early in the morning and walk all day in the mountains. The long evenings in each other's company, the prayers spoken in the quiet of the country nights, the Mass shared at a portable altar in some beautiful spot all contribute to create an 'atmosphere' which favours the unfolding of the community spirit. Other times we don't leave the town till Sunday morning and return late the same evening.

Of course prudent people warn me against the dangers and temptations such a grouping of young men and girls might entail, particularly living in such great spiritual intimacy. Although I cannot vouch for the future I can truthfully say that at present the community is a model of perfect purity and I have not heard a single word or seen the least sign

49

which would indicate otherwise. It seems that even the temptation to flirt can get no foothold in our community. I cannot tell whether it is by special grace that the relations between us have been from the beginning very simple and truly fraternal but certainly our way of life in the 'community' has stressed and brought out the best in every member. Of course I should not be surprised if a number of the young people in the group were to marry each other—but after all what's wrong with that? The very first members included couples engaged to be married.

5th August

It has been suggested it would be better if I left Marseilles for a while. The Germans have arrested some of my friends and searched others. So I have chosen a large village in the mountains for a temporary home.

I first spent 48 hours in a little country town and, wanting to make a telephone call, entered the first café I came to. The people in the café looked at me as if I had thrown a bomb and it was only later that I found out why—the café was Protestant owned and I had gone in wearing my cassock. Apparently in that town half the population is Catholic and half Protestant and contact between the two denominations is practically non-existent. Each faction has its own grocers, hairdressers, cafés, and schools. They don't speak to each other, either because they don't know each other or because they pretend not to do so.

This village is a hundred per cent Catholic and yesterday, Sunday, the church was packed to capacity at every Mass. The parish priest assured me it was always the same and in fact one would need a great deal of courage and a total disregard for public opinion to stay away from Mass or, for that matter, from vespers. But I was surprised to see that very few of the faithful used a missal. Some of them quietly said their beads but others were openly dreaming until 'it was all over' as Claudel once put it. I could see no response at all to my sermon probably because I cannot speak to these country people in the realistic and descriptive style Christ, in his inimitable way, spoke to his hearers.

Saturday evening after the parish priest had deliberately and very openly left the village for a long walk I had a large crowd round the confessional. They all wanted to avail themselves of the rare occasion when a stranger could hear their confessions without knowing anything of their personal lives. Many Catholics think their personal sins are so unusual that they must necessarily make a lasting impression on the priest and some penitents are afraid of being despised if the priest is allowed to glimpse the state of their soul—which is why in towns those who work in close contact with the priest rarely go to him for confession. Here where there is only one church in a radius of many miles the advent of a strange priest is a godsend and the people make full use of it. And yet—adultery, petty theft, detraction of one's neighbour, lies . . . the same sins as everywhere else.

7th August

The villagers are very proud of their 'high moral standard' and since I came I have been told at least once a day that there are only two unmarried mothers in the whole parish. Unfortunately the act by which a girl can become an unmarried mother occurs much more frequently but as it is not done openly in broad daylight it does not affect their 'moral' susceptibilities. As for the pharisaical pride with which they speak about the unmarried mothers—no one seems to think that this too might possibly offend against 'morality'. It is the bigots who more than any others constitute themselves an argument for Dr Freud's plea for unrestrained yielding to sex impulses.

8th August

I miss no opportunity to have a word with the 'simple' people and if need be I go out of my way to start conversation with them. The world of these rather rough and ready country

folk is quite new to me; many traits of character are here revealed in their natural state whereas in the towns they are
distorted or disguised under the cloak of 'good behaviour'.

The older generation disapproves of the younger generation
and while this is common everywhere the reasons alleged here
are somewhat unexpected. 'They are only Catholics in name'
the old say of the young. Now two miles from this hundred
per cent Catholic village, at the foot of the hill, there is a
Protestant village but from the way the inhabitants live totally
ignoring each other one would think they were hundreds of
miles apart. If they meet on the road or in the market of the
local town they take no notice of each other and pretend to be
strangers. They never inter-marry and never help each other in
need. I am told that when, a few years ago, a fire destroyed a
number of farms in our village not a single person from the
neighbouring village made the least move to come to help;
and although there is an unwritten law in the countryside
about these things which is very strong yet the people in this
village would not have acted differently. But today the religious
antipathy between the two villages has slowed down and
become passive rather than active—and that, believe it or not,
is the grievance the old people have against the younger
generation. They tell me how 'in the old days', after a pint or
two the young people of our village used to arm themselves
with sticks and stones and descend on the 'Hugenot' village
each Saturday evening—and their eyes shine when they recall
the splendid battles they used to fight 'for the glory of the
Virgin Mother and the true religion'. But they admit that at
other times they were forced to defend themselves because the
young Hugenots were no less belligerent.

10th August

I have heard so much about the hostilities between Catholic
and Protestant in this region that yesterday, feeling that
somebody must do something about it, I went to visit the
Protestant minister. He couldn't hide his astonishment but it

was his parisioners who were worried when they saw, for the first time in living memory, a priest entering their rectory. All the time I was there they hung about outside the door in case they were needed to intervene. Evidently a papist could only have evil designs on their minister; they have never heard of the ecumenical movement and have no idea of the genuinely friendly relations which usually exist in towns between the Church and Christians of other denominations. In this part of the country religious wars are by no means past history.

12th August

I have just had a lesson after all the things I have said and thought about country people and the way their religion is choked with superstition. The parish priest went away for a few days leaving me in charge to deal with any urgent matters. It wasn't long before I was summoned to the bed of a dying woman who lived in a hamlet about three or four miles from the presbytery. After the custom of the country I put on surplice and stole, took the ciborium and set out preceded by a young countryman who carried a lantern and rang a bell. It was pouring with rain but from every house we passed on the way the people came out and knelt in the mud adoring Christ in the eucharist. There was something both noble and moving in their time-honoured action and it made me more deeply conscious of my mission to bring God to them.

When I got to the hamlet and spoke to the old lady—she was about 75—I took it for granted she was afraid of death and tried to give her courage by telling her that maybe her illness was not so dangerous after all and there was a chance she might be up and about in a few weeks. To my amazement she said: 'Father why do you want to take away my joy? I am very old and I have been ill for a long time. I have worked hard and suffered a lot and when I think that this very night I shall be reunited with Jesus and his Mother, my parents and my children who died before me, I am truly happy.' And then she proceeded to tell me about heaven. To her it was not only the hope on which she had staked her life but as real and familiar a place as her own courtyard. And she had no knowledge of theology and her religion had consisted of saying her rosary—more or less absent-mindedly—while she was washing dishes or milking cows, and in lighting candles in front of the statues of our Lady and St Anthony. I left her with tears in my eyes, deeply touched by her intense and sincere faith. How paltry intellectual discussion seems in the presence of simple and living faith.

20th August

The priests in charge of these mountain parishes take a very stern view of their duties. As well as preaching the gospel and administering the sacraments they conceive it their duty to act as guardian of public morals and usually carry this so far that they end by policing their flock rather than ministering to them.

Yesterday I was at a village twenty-five miles from here and was surprised to find so few young people either in church or in the fields. The local school teacher explained to me that the parish priest refuses to allow either a cinema or regular dances in his parish. A few years ago a travelling cinema came, as they do to remote regions, and from the pulpit the priest threatened his flock with damnation if they dared visit the cinema which according to him is an instrument of hell. Except for a few die-hards nobody went near—possibly less from fear of hell than of those 'good Christians' who stood guard over the doors ready to report any lapses to the priest so that he could denounce them by name the following Sunday. Incidentally that is how he deals with young couples who attend dances in the neighbouring villages. Small wonder that as soon as they have the opportunity the young people join the services or go off to factories in the towns.

I felt I had to make quite sure whether or not the teacher was exaggerating so I mentioned the subject to the parish

54

priest. Alas he was so vehement in his insistence that modern amusements are occasions of sin that I was forced to believe the teacher had been speaking the exact truth.

23rd August

Popes and theologians remind us time after time that the holy sacrifice of the Mass is the supreme prayer of Christians and that it is Christ who offers himself in the Mass and who guides the prayer. But to see some priests one would hardly think so. Many hurry through the Mass mumbling the names of the deceased for whom the faithful are asked to pray; they preach less about God than about money and politics and finally, after pronouncing the *Ite Missa est* they step down from the altar and announce 'And now brethren let us pray'. Then come strings of 'Our Father's and 'Hail Mary's for the intention of the Holy Father, for the leaders of the country and the benefactors of the parish. One cannot really wonder if the faithful prefer to say the rosary during Mass rather than use a missal. But I was wrong apparently to attribute this disregard for the dignity of the Mass to the priests—apparently they carry out to the letter the instructions of their bishops!

5th October

We, the priests of the resistance, try hard to get our bishops to see how much their decrees disturb seminarists and young members of Catholic action. The Vichy government urges these young people to comply with the German order for compulsory work in armaments factories etc. and, except for a very few, most bishops have urged their people to 'follow the directives of the legitimate power'. Seminarists even interrupt their studies and are moved to Germany to turn out shells. And we cannot convince the bishops that a government which is so restricted in its decisions cannot be truly considered 'legitimate' or that orders issued by a foreign occupying power cannot morally compel obedience. How can men who are so experienced in religious matters be so ignorant of elementary temporal facts. A few days ago I visited one prelate and tried to explain about the increasing reluctance of people to collaborate with the Germans. He refused to believe me—assured me he was well-informed about the people's reactions and state of mind. Who informs him? Presumably his Vicars General, the youngest of whom is in his seventies; they in their turn presumably cull their information from their house-keepers.

The lack of liaison between the hierarchy and the world is probably the main cause of the Church's slow grasp of what is happening to the world. It is not a question of mishandling a temporary political situation—the bishops are mostly genuinely unaware of the real nature of the problems of the apostolate and the spiritual anguish of this generation. One Cardinal of Paris realised some years ago that his courtiers would not supply him with the kind of information he most needed and he formed the practice of inviting to dinner the priests from the poorest parishes and those in the thick of the fight who had the courage to tell him the truth; moreover he invited laymen also in order to hear their point of view. I don't know what effect this venture has had but I do know that something of the sort is badly needed in these dioceses of the south.

3rd November

Considering the bishops' attitude towards the duties of Catholics and the 'legitimate powers' one can't help admiring the courage of those priests and laypeople who join the re-sistance. One bishop indeed severely reprimanded a young priest for admitting frankly that he was a de Gaullist. Yet the bishop cannot see that he must take a consistent attitude—either he must impose his own political views on the priest in the name of ecclesiastical discipline or he must ignore his informers.

4th November

Nothing revolts me more than to see good people playing the informer. If ever a priest expresses himself a little too freely or criticises certain practices and customs there is bound to be

56

someone who will report what he has said—usually misquoting him—to the bishop or one of the Vicars General.

Although I am on the best of terms with the headmistress of the school where I teach social science it doesn't prevent her reporting to the bishop every nonconformist statement I make in the course of my teaching. Last week, speaking about capitalist speculation, I used as an example the case of the shipowner who sells, reacquires and resells his ship while it is peacefully ploughing the seas. Apparently my example touched a well-known local Catholic on the raw—and the headmistress rushed to tell the bishop about my appalling lapse in taste. Poor bishop.

The worst part is these informers act with the best of intentions and convinced they are working for the greater glory of God and the welfare of souls and, of course, above all for the soul of the priest in question. It is frightening how much evil is perpetrated under the heading 'doing good'. The Marxists obviously exaggerate when they insist on a completely 'objective' attitude—but the subjectivism of Catholics is hardly less monstrous.

1944

3rd March
A friend of mine told me about a certain parish priest who would be willing to help the resistance movement and the new guerilla forces we are forming. I went to see him and found him living in the most distressing conditions I have ever known a priest live in. He was ordained two years ago and put in charge of a small country parish in a predominantly Protestant part. Fewer than thirty out of three hundred Catholics come to the Sunday Mass and there is only one man among them. In the week there is no one to assist the priest and he celebrates Mass alone in a church which in winter is icy. The only people in the whole district he could have an

intelligent conversation with are two teachers and the doctor and all three are fiercely anti-clerical and flatly refuse to have anything to do with him. Often weeks go by without his exchanging so much as a greeting with anyone. Of course there are other priests in this district—but the nearest parish is twelve miles away and this young priest isn't strong enough to cycle so far and is too poor to be able to entertain one of the others if they came to see him. I found him in a terrible state of tension, discouragement and despair and I am not sure whether he will be able to pull himself together.

Our bishops expect filial devotion from their priests—which is as it should be—yet the bishop of this diocese has never bothered to go and see this priest or find out what sort of conditions he lives in. True there is a petrol shortage, yet this particular bishop—who comes from a 'good' family— feels it his duty to drive once every month to his home three hundred miles away to bless the marriages and preside at ceremonies among the local gentry so he can hardly have much petrol left for visiting his poor priests. The resistance is planning to purge the civil service—but what can be done to purge the civil service of the Church?

4th March

I have worried so much that at last I decided I ought to write to the bishop and tell him of the desperate plight of this young—and very courageous—priest but I haven't much hope that my letter will produce any practical result.

8th April

I haven't mentioned the 'community' for some time but it is nevertheless thriving and active and there is a junior 'community' of younger members who meet their elders for Mass and occasionally join in a week-end outing. Altogether there are more than thirty members now and their determination to live a truly Christian life is stronger than ever. Last year some of them finished their studies and their main concern is how they can live an adult life based not on the usual ideals of success and material advantage and social status but on Christian values, choosing their jobs according to the opportunities they offer for apostolic work. A few older men from various professions have joined us giving us a wider outlook although fundamentally their preoccupation is not very different from that of the young people. One owns a factory and wants to try to lead his workers in the spirit of the group; another is a banker and a third an engineer and they all realise they must revolutionise their relations with their subordinates. Yesterday, Good Friday, we made a real 'Way of the Cross' carrying a large wooden cross from the town to Notre Dame de la Garde and kneeling in the road for the prayers. Heads appeared at windows all along the way but it seemed to me significant that no one ridiculed or insulted us—some old sweepers even raised their caps as we passed. I can't help thinking that what impressed people was that the penitents were not from the ranks of the elderly bigots they are accustomed to think of as 'representing' religion but were all young and patently sincere. Of course we shall be accused of sensationalism and causing 'scandal'; but how can we rouse the people from their inertia except by shock treatment?

17th August

At present I am in a country town and one of the local bigwigs, a textile owner and prominent local Catholic, invited me to dinner. I don't know him personally and he only knows about me because at one time I instructed one of his daughters. I soon discovered he had not invited me because he felt any personal sympathy towards me. He has been a devoted follower of Marshal Pétain and made quite an active contribution towards the Vichy government. His factory employs only women and if he discovered that the husband or son or brother of any of his workers had refused to go to work in Germany he immediately sacked the woman in question. Now, of course, since the allied landing, he is scared. His brother who acted in much the same way has already been arrested by one of the guerilla bands whose tribunals are known to be far from gentle with collaborators. My host wants me to help him and is doing his best to convince me that he acted in good faith for the welfare of the Church and for France. I don't doubt his sincerity—but I can't help wondering whether stupidity is an excuse for crime.

The trouble is this is by no means a rare case. We shall have our work cut out in the near future to prevent the communists alleging that the Church in France has been the main accomplice of the Vichy government. Fortunately there are a few men like Fr Chaillet, Fr Maydieu, Georges Bidault and the Archbishop of Toulouse—and any number of obscure priests and laymen—who have upheld the honour of the Church during these dark years.

19th August

This morning I attended the strangest ceremony outside the town hall. The local guerillas have elected a very brisk inspector to be in charge of the district's liberation and an impressive number of armed fighters turned up for the ceremony. It is interesting to wonder where they have sprung from—until 15th August the guerilla force of the whole neighbourhood numbered only about ten men most of whom had refused service under Vichy. Now practically every young man in the district, particularly the communists and those who had been loudest in praise of M. Pétain, was on parade, armed to the teeth with parachuted British and American tommy guns. I was musing bitterly about it while the new leader addressed the assembly when suddenly the rumour spread 'The Germans are coming back'. In less than a minute the square was empty, the rostrum deserted, I and the two girls who had accompanied me being among the last to leave. The neo-guerilla fighters were in such haste that they flung their weapons away as they ran. I had an inspiration—I went to look for the local headmaster. He had confided to me earlier that he was frightened for his life because he had instructed his scouts to set a good example by supporting the government and going to work in Germany. Together we collected all the discarded weapons and hid them in a shed near the school. If at some future time the pseudo-guerillas try to make him out a collaborator I shall be able to prove that he rendered at least one valuable service to the resistance. We had hardly finished when the first soldiers marched in—Americans! Tonight we shall have to return the weapons.

3rd September

This morning I went to Marseilles which has just been liberated—a German tank, burnt out, stands in front of the bishop's house. This bishop is of course in an awkward position. In spite of various warnings from the resistance he insisted on presiding at the requiem for one of the Vichy ministers whom the resistance killed, and preached a panegyric. Communists and socialists and various members of the liberation commission are trying to use this as an excuse to have him removed, but although this has happened in some dioceses where the priests have made no move to help their bishop, here in Marseilles the resistance priests have been loud in defence of their bishop. They pointed out that although he disapproved of the resistance he never acted against it and never hesitated to use his authority to protect resistance priests from the police. But he has been advised to keep to his house and stay away from the thanksgiving celebrations. In a few days people will have calmed down.

4th December

Three months only since the liberation, the war is still on and most of the members of our 'community' have been called up—and yet already all the old feuds are starting up all over again. In the last months of the occupation we often discussed the type of government France should adopt when she was free. We rarely agreed because some of us preferred an authoritarian regime like that of Salazar with a Christian basis, whereas others favoured a socialist democracy. But we were unanimous that whatever happened we must avoid at all costs a return to the dead sea of the 'people's republic'. However little we loved Vichy no one mourned the passing of the third republic. We frequently talked to young people who held very different views from our own but they all—communists, socialists, resistance workers, held the same belief in the rebirth of our country though I had little doubt in my own mind what sort of birth the communists were hoping for. But they are a minority and the vast majority never doubted that the future France would be free and ruled by justice and brotherhood. True in London—and later in Algiers—the generals and politicians of the old school hatched their intrigues in the best traditions of the caricature of democracy which we believed we should never see again. We were sure we were strong enough to prevent them 'poisoning' the new France. Well I returned from my first trip to liberated Paris a short while ago. For the first few days I was happy in the knowledge that decent men once again occupied responsible government posts; I even met a friend from the resistance who has been given ministerial responsibility and is determined to revolutionise the political principles of this country. But my joy was short-lived. I had of course no chance to penetrate to high places but even what I saw convinced me that we are not going to find it easy to rid this country not only of the traces of the Nazi occupation but also of the political past which was responsible for the occupation having taken place. The politicians of the old regime whom we were convinced had disappeared for ever are turning up again everywhere, rising to the top, determined as always not to miss their opportunity.

And even here in Marseilles the old quarrels and rivalries are springing up again. The communists are managing to organise their cells in the very organisations created by the underground in a spirit of general agreement. The socialists seem only concerned about getting power and well paid jobs. And how do the Christians react to all this? Will they be able to rise above the ghetto-mentality which has so sorely afflicted them in the past?

All my fellow Christians who had not been content to accept Vichy domination were determined that they should. Was not the deplorable state of the third republic before the occupation partly due to the childish attitude of the Christian masses refusing to acknowledge that social progress was both inevitable and essential for the welfare of the country? When it was too late they sat in judgment on the republic and democracy as such. True there were organisations and movements among dynamically minded Catholics but they were not supported by the majority. Most turned their eyes backwards and dreamed of a sort of medieval revival. And in spite of all the resolution it seems as though the ghetto complex is firmly rooted in the mind of twentieth-century Catholics. They only feel safe among themselves. They are sure the 'others' are probably stronger and wicked and they maintain that it is better to avoid contact with 'unbelievers' so as not to be infected by bad example. There are among us many left wing Christians who would like to join forces, politically, with other progressive parties. In our contact with the guerilla forces and the deported men in prison camps we had plenty of opportunity to see that our ideas on the organisation of the temporal world were much more in tune with those of the atheistic progressive parties than with the greater part of our co-religionists who were anxiously upholding the principles of the old social structures.

Obviously I don't share the illusion of some of my friends who believe an honest and loyal co-operation with the communists is possible—I have had far too much insight into communist aims and methods for that. Undoubtedly no one can work sincerely with the communists on one plane and yet retain their independence in all other spheres of thought. The communists merely use joint meetings as a method of preparing lists of non-communists who might be susceptible to party indoctrination. What else after all can one expect? Every communist believes that he is in possession of a sort of revealed truth and certainly of absolute truth regarding social, economic and political organisation. Their position within the left wing movements is in some ways analogous to that of many Catholics who pray for Church unity but are quite unable to conceive this unity in any terms other than complete conversion of all Christian denominations to the Church.

But what about the genuine socialists, particularly the younger generation? And the many people who have no definite political leanings but who, during the fight for freedom, discovered an aim in life and who agree with us that there would have been little point in driving out the Germans without being determined to create a new France. Why can we not all form a workers' movement inspired by the best traditions of socialism? Since we believe the social revolution to be inevitable why do we have to wait until it is brought about by totalitarian adepts?

The usual objection is that many socialists and people with left wing leanings are atheists. Certainly this atheism exists among them but need it prevent us from working together for the betterment of the temporal world?

I do not mean to say that there are two distinct spheres of existence for Christians, one depending on faith and concerned with divine matters and the other based on political convictions and dealing with temporal matters. Such a division would be totally unrealistic and moreover we of the left wing have too often accused 'traditionalist' Christians of that error to succumb to it now ourselves. The Christian must give of his best—which is his faith—in order to play his part in the construction of the human world. But would it not be possible to work hand in hand, on the purely practical level, with those who don't believe in a heaven yet are prepared to give of their best in order to make this world a happier and more beautiful place to live in? I have often discussed this question with young socialists and it seems that the anti-clericalism which their party used to propagate is as alien to them as the clericalism of former generations is to us. I cannot see why we should not pool our resources and mobilise our combined strength to serve the aims of human liberation and advancement about which we more or less agree. Then French socialists would not only stand a good chance of forming the vanguard of a social revolution but could also help to lead a free Europe towards those high aims, since the English labour party has become so bogged in the swamps of conformism that it can no longer galvanise the people into action. From the reports I have received it seems that the Vatican and the French bishops expect leaders of Catholic laity and those of the popular democracy to form a denominational party more or less on the lines of the Catholic parties of Belgium, Holland and Germany. The ecclesiastical authorities are said to fear that should the Catholic socialists join a party of left wing leanings they would be swallowed up by the party's policy instead of upholding the 'supreme interests' of their religion. Evidently the authorities are not so concerned about the Christians who belong to the right wing parties, although they are as little specifically religious minded as their left wing brethren and, moreover, are under the leadership of quite a number of atheists and freemasons. Is the lively spirit of the Church in France to be imprisoned again a new ghetto?

18th December

The ecclesiastical authorities have given me a sharp rebuke for having spoken at a meeting against the revival of a Catholic syndicalism and for advocating democratic and non-denominational syndicalism . . .

1945 — 8

1945

3rd March

Ever since the liberation the main preoccupation of the progressive Catholics seems to have been whether or not it is possible to work with the communists; only a very few Catholics have paid attention to the call for collaboration with left wing liberals and the socialists. Could it be that the best among the Catholic laity feel, perhaps even without knowing it, that the structure of the Church and that of communism are in some ways alike? It is useless to deny that the two organisations have things in common—dogmatism for example and unswerving obedience to authority and the strict discipline. But it seems to me there are more reasons for this sympathy than meet the eye.

The young Catholic generation especially having seen only too clearly the awful results of the *laissez-faire* in the Christian attitude towards the common run of mankind in the past is eager to make reparation. The communist movement being apparently the most 'progressive', the young Catholics are afraid to condemn it in case in future their children should accuse them of being 'reactionary' as they now accuse their elders.

I am often asked nowadays to speak on communism at public meetings, Catholic Action groups and various chaplains' gatherings. Now I do not believe in the possibility of an honest co-operation with the communists. The methods they use and the aims they pursue are so diametrically opposed to one of the most fundamental principles of Christian philosophy, the respect of the human being, that it is impossible to subscribe to communism without betraying Christianity. But at the same time I try to distinguish between the unfortunate consequences of their policy and the total negation of their ideals which so many Christians profess. I don't believe in the party's promises but I can see the greatness and the single-mindedness of the masses who adhere to it and I often quote the words of Ber-diaeff: 'Communism bears witness to the duties which Christianity has failed to fulfil.' All the various propaganda tricks invented to counteract the growing influence of communism on the masses are downright childish. It seems to me that communism is an evil not so much because it is too revolutionary but because, on the contrary, it is not revolutionary enough. The only method by which Christians can solve the dilemma of choosing between a communist and a conservative policy is to turn the tables on the communists and outstrip them in their 'revolutionary' ideas, not just to create upheavals but to become the leaven of the world of which Christ spoke when he charged his disciples to spread his message.

9th May

Henry, the delegate of Marseilles Catholic youth in the young communists' executive committee is on the best of terms with the local communist president and regards him as a friend, and has every reason to believe the regard is mutual. Yet a few days ago the president who knew that Henry, as a Catholic, could not approve a resolution to be put before the committee, salved his conscience by omitting to invite Henry to the meeting. Somehow I have got to make Henry see that whereas this kind of behaviour is completely inadmissible from the point of view of Christian morality, it is a perfectly legitimate thing for a communist to do because in his eyes everything, including friendship, is subject to the interests of the party. There is no reason to doubt the communist's sincerity—but the incident serves to show how difficult the situation really is.

16th May

Recently during a meeting of chaplains to workers' organisations I was asked to give a clear exposition of the attitude which Christians ought to take in the event of a communist victory

70

at the next election. Many people think such a victory is possible and I am not wholly convinced they are wrong.

After carefully explaining that what I was going to say was simply my very personal opinion I went on to tell them that it would be no solution either to cold-shoulder the regime or to oppose it actively from the start. We should have to apply the methods the Church recommends to her ministers when they are in charge of Christians living under any of the other political regimes. We must put our entire strength at the disposal of society, doing our best to alleviate its miseries but firmly refusing to comply with anything directly opposed to the Christian conscience. Such a situation would obviously be a very difficult one but then is not the position of every Christian in the world necessarily difficult? No political regime is ever perfect in Christian terms so why should communism be an exception—why decide in advance that it must deprive us utterly of any chance of fulfilling our mission to bear witness to Christ?

Now these chaplains regard temporal affairs very much as I do and most of them therefore agreed with me. But I feel that people in general don't understand what is involved.

From various sources I have learned that the rumour is spreading in this part of France that through my agency 'Rome' has given instructions that its priests are not to fight communism. So I have succeeded in being looked upon as the official spokesman of the Vatican! But of course I never intended to 'give instructions' to anybody, nor to propagate a lenient attitude towards communism. I am far too much aware of the dangers it entails for the Church and for mankind to be anything but wholeheartedly opposed to the attitude with which I am charged. At the meeting I referred to it was simply a question of facing up to the possibility of the communists gaining power in spite of our opposition.

7th June

M. is a strange man. During the occupation, as a young

71

university lecturer and secretary of the YCW, he showed the most reckless courage. In 1940 he led the opposition at Lyons to the showing of the Nazi version of the film *Jew Suss*. In his lectures he didn't hesitate to denounce the Vichy government and speak openly of his hopes for allied victory. He helped found and distribute *Témoinage Chrétien*, the underground paper, and became in fact a sort of Christian hero of the resistance. It was almost a miracle that in spite of total disregard for his own safety he avoided the clutches of both the Gestapo and the army for the four years of the occupation. During all that time he missed no opportunity to point out to the bishops and the ecclesiastical authorities how wrong they were to accept favours offered by the Vichy regime and to give it moral support and today he reminds them of the mistakes they made on every possible occasion.

A week ago M. spoke at a meeting. Afterwards during the dinner the local bishop had the place of honour and in his speech he praised the work of the 'Christian resistance'. In his reply M. rudely (perhaps too rudely) reminded him of a number of his pastoral letters which had glorified the Pétain regime and of the severe sanctions he had applied against one particular Gaullist priest. And yesterday, speaking to the Archbishop of his region, M. exclaimed almost in the voice of a prophet: 'Monsignor, humble yourself and admit your errors. Had it not been for some of your priests and laypeople having the courage to disobey you for four whole years neither you nor the majority of your bishops would now occupy your palaces.'

This kind of address must stupefy anyone accustomed to ecclesiastical language but fundamentally what M. said is true and perhaps it is no bad thing that for once an active layman should tell a prominent leader of the Church, who normally hears little except praise, the plain unvarnished truth.

16th August

I am not much addicted to pilgrimages. No doubt this is

partly because I am a convert and as such always feel embarrassed at public demonstrations of the Catholic faith. But my aversion is also due to the things one sees in the famous pilgrimage centres. The way in which religion is commercialised in these places is enough to sicken anyone. I know the Church doesn't profit from it—but why does she tolerate it? She certainly has authority enough to drive the traders from the temple—and even from the vicinity of the temple—if she made up her mind to do so. Moreover I have often been forced to see that in some places—particularly in this sunny part of the south of France—pilgrimages are often regarded as a sort of bargain with God. But does any man seriously believe that because he has been to Lourdes or to Notre Dame de la Garde or has passed a night in vigil in front of some relic or other that he is therefore 'quits' with God? The spiritual directors of most Catholic Action groups condemn spectacular demonstrations of faith because of the harm they can do to their work.

So if I have agreed to go to La Salette with some friends it is not so much the pilgrimage to our Lady which draws me as my admiration of Leon Bloy who had a very special devotion to our Lady of La Salette. Every summer many people who directly or indirectly owe a great deal to Leon Bloy go to La Salette and I see no reason why I shouldn't join them. At the seminary when I was tired of religious formalism and weary of the arid manner in which some of our teachers presented theology I always returned to Bloy's works. They gave me the courage I needed to persevere. A few of his disciples whom I had the privilege of meeting struck me as among the liveliest members of the Church in France.

*   *   *

And how glad I am that I went. As a site La Salette is incomparably more beautiful than Lourdes. From the village of

C*   73

Corps a sort of tractor, the only means of transport, climbs up the hill. Riding in this vehicle is itself a penance and it may be the reason tourists have not yet invaded La Salette. But what most pleased me was that the trade in pious objects is on so small a scale and done so discreetly that one is scarcely aware of it. And although I went to La Salette in search of Bloy it was our Lady I found there. And I realised that perhaps I was too scathing about Lourdes and pilgrimages in general—perhaps most Christians who go find God in spite of the traders.

18th August

After leaving La Salette I went to the Grande Chartreuse. What particularly impressed me was the extraordinary beauty of the Alpine scenery. (And it is all I am going to say about La Chartreuse itself because one day I hope to go again.) We ascended via Voiron and came back via St Pierre. In the course of my travels over many parts of the world I have seen a great number of very beautiful landscapes but to me none of them can compare with the sheer splendour of La Chartreuse. And it is in this unique spot, of all places, that the most austere among all Catholic religious Orders has its roots.

In fact it seems that most of the old monasteries were built on magnificent sites and I don't think it is coincidence that their saintly founders chose them in preference to more modest places. The pious and insipid 'lives' of the saints have misrepresented their real character to such an extent that, to us, they often appear to have been indifferent, if not actually hostile, to all beauty in their preoccupation with heavenly splendours. But the gospel tells how susceptible our Lord was to the beauty of the created world and I can't help wondering why we had to experience the horrors of the reformation, counter-reformation and Jansenism (the effects of which are still discernible in the unconscious mind of many Christians) if the majority of pious people think of this world only as 'vale of tears' and are convinced they must enjoy its treasures as little as possible. It is self-evident that we must not adore the things of this world; but we can and ought to admire them because they are the reflection of the ineffable beauty of God.

20th October

H. and I were asked to speak on behalf of the Christian Evidence movement at a mass meeting organised jointly by Christian Evidence and the National Front at a cinema in Arles. A lawyer and another man were to speak for the National Front. The hall was packed—according to our local friends about one-third of the audience was Catholic and the other two-thirds either pro-communist or party members.

The meeting had been inspired by the resistance movement in an attempt to unite its members in a spirit of brotherhood. The lawyer, very ingeniously, tried to convince the Catholics that they have nothing to fear from collaboration with communism, H. spoke about the revolutionary ambitions of young Christians and I voiced the doubts and hesitations the Catholics feel about accepting the communists' outstretched hand. But in spite of all we could do to start a general discussion the audience were quite determined to stick to the old quarrel and it was quite evident they didn't really listen to what was being said. What the spokesman for the National Front said was cheered by his followers and hissed by the Catholics— and in the same way whatever H. and I said was cheered by the Catholics and booed by the communists.

My own speech was not popular with the all-too-clever lawyer who was the spokesman for the National Front. However much I try to water down my argument the fact always emerges that to my mind atheism, the basic principle of communism, is the main obstacle to co-operation between Christians and communists. The lawyer, deliberately misunderstanding me, tried to make out that we Catholics are determined to undermine every attempt at unity the communists make and further tried to answer me by 'proving' that communism

75

is only atheist because the Church supports the exploiters and the reactionaries and that sincerely progressive Christians would have no more difficulty in practising their faith within the cell of the communist part than they have in the framework of a dictator state. There were quite a number of red Spaniards in the audience who broke into frenzied clamour every time the lawyer mentioned apostolic blessings bestowed on General Franco. I knew quite well that the lawyer's arguments would sound plausible to many young Christians. Even a well educated boy like Henry half believes in the 'historical' cause of atheism being one of communism's principles and the young priest we had had dinner with had expressed a similar view. So at all costs I had to demonstrate that communism is not merely hostile to Christianity for social and political reason but that it is radically and inseparably bound up with atheism. Fortunately I had brought with me a series of official speeches on atheism by the communist leaders and was thus able to attack the lawyer with the very words of his communist gods. I accused him of distorting the doctrine of Lenin and Stalin, of being a 'heretic'. The audience got confused—time after time I was cheered by the communists while the Catholics were obviously at a loss to know what it was all about. Neither party knew sufficient about Marxist doctrine to be able to follow the argument between the lawyer and myself—the only impression they could get was that I was apparently defending the atheistic and materialistic Marxism of Lenin against the lawyer who had deviated from the 'truth'.

The meeting broke up in complete confusion and the lawyer was furious with me.

21st October

The bishop sent for me because early this morning the police called to tell him that last night in Arles I had publicly committed myself to the communist party. It only took me a few minutes to explain what had happened and we both laughed and wondered at the stupidity of police informers.

9th March

Marseilles society has been electrified by the sensational news that Frère Jacques, the Dominican docker, has succeeded in convincing the bishop that an officially authorised team of 'working' missionaries within the framework of the parish is a matter of urgent need. It is to replace the individual social workers who at the best of times are only tolerated by ecclesiastical authority.

The bishop has entrusted to the missionary team the vast working parish of St Louis, one of the outlying suburbs of Marseilles. To begin with it is to have five resident priests under a superior with Fr Jacques as the brain behind the scenes. One of Fr Jacques' revolutionary notions is his refusal to accept the traditional separation of secular and religious priests, still less the separation of religious of various Orders. As a latecomer to the priesthood he has had plenty of opportunity of seeing the petty quarrels and childish jealousies between various factions of the clergy and has realised how they harm the reputation of the Church. How can people believe in the gospel message of love when priests, consecrated in one and the same Church, indulge in petty and sectarian quarrels? Fr Jacques' idea is that secular priests and Dominicans, Jesuits, Franciscans and others should work together in a spirit of fraternity without one being 'superior' to the other. A short circular sent to all the residents of St Louis reads: 'The five priests who have come to live among you are not after your money, nor do they constitute a fifth column of capitalist reactionaries. Because they love God and love you they have come here to share your worries and your hopes, and without any ulterior motive they want to help you whenever they can.' Then follows a few personal details—Fr G. is from a working class family, Fr L. is a lawyer who became a priest at 27, and so on.

The working population of St Louis gave the mission a great welcome—in strong contrast to the anything but friendly reception from the majority of the practising Catholics (approximately 500) in the parish. They are mostly lower middle class, they cling to tradition and oppose every 'innovation' particularly when it affects their religious habits. The reaction of the diocesan clergy is on the whole hostile—they maintain that the mission priests are out to 'teach them their job'. And the fact that the mission has banned collections during Mass and has abolished 'classified' weddings and funerals has given rise to the rumour that the priests have secret monetary resources. Fr Jacques himself is accused of boasting that he has 'lived a wordly life'—although the extraordinary humility of this apostle of dockers and rag-and-bone men ought to be obvious to everybody.

Whit Sunday

Our 'community' has camped at Riboux in beautiful surroundings at the foot of the St Baume range. We are the only inhabitants of the little village which was abandoned some years ago because the water supply fails at certain times in the year. The houses are deserted except for birds and animals sheltering in them and it is a very long time since the church door was opened. But since at this time of year water is plentiful we have camped on the village green for the next few days.

The young people's joy and quiet happiness defies description; even the most wordly and flirtatious of the girls have changed into simple and natural human beings. We get up very early, dress quickly and are ready when the bell (put in order by one of our engineers) rings for Mass. Then we spend the day praying and studying together, doing the chores, walking and in the evening sitting together round the camp fire. Some of the members, half joking but half serious said how dreary the prospect is of leaving this idyllic existence and going back to everyday life and the terrible problems of trying not to compromise their Christian principles in the

78

middle of the evil and the impurity in the materialistic world. They would far rather stay here at Riboux and live permanently in a simple brotherly community. Indeed one girl, the daughter of a wealthy industrialist, has just offered me her dowry to purchase the whole village of Riboux. Of course I enjoyed building these castles in the air as much as anyone and of course I long as much as they do to live among such true and sincere friends. And indeed we all know that there are already in France a number of communities whose ideals are similar to ours and who actually lead the type of life we hanker for. Practically there is nothing much to prevent us following their example and turning our back on the life of the towns. Since the community was formed three years ago we have shared intense joy and peace and our pilgrimages, camps and meetings have been like stages in an experience of what we consider real life and we naturally find it difficult to fit in a world which conforms so little to our idea of life as a Christian should live it. But why should this longing for a rural and secluded life be so strong just now? Three years ago we had no wish to retire from worldly activities. True we planned a communal life but we intended to live it in the midst of the town and to have a full share of the conflicts and strife of the world. During 1943 and '44 we looked forward to living in a free France. It took less than two years to disillusion us about that and today no one any longer believes that we are on the threshold of a great and genuine revolution. The older members among us have to cope with the endless problems of everyday life and the younger ones have somehow to resist the temptation to join in and be carried away by the maelstrom of amusements, pleasures and ambitions to which the youth of the country is succumbing. How wrong it is to maintain that suffering necessarily ennobles human nature. After years of privation and anxiety the young people in France are concerned solely to make up for lost time and have no other thought than to live in a frenzy of 'enjoying themselves' at a pace twice and three times as fast as they can stand. The young people in our community are afraid of not being strong enough to withstand the onslaught—that is the real reason they want to leave and break with a world which is in such sharp contrast to their ideals. They want the community as a refuge.

As a result of this probing of conscience we find the strength to give up this nostalgia for the simple life here in Riboux. As a matter of fact if we had really seriously considered the project we should I think have found it impossible to carry out. The ties by which most of us are attached to the world are infinitely stronger than we like to admit and moreover we have so often spoken of our duty to be present in the world that the mere serious discussion of evading it underlines how we are betraying our ideals.

14th June

In an article on communism in a special number of *Témoinage Chrétien* I violently attacked the opportunism of the communist party. I maintained that the reason Christians cannot belong to the party is not its revolutionary programme but the fact, obvious to any dispassionate observer, that the party is basically and hopelessly reactionary in its aims. The communist party wants a revolution but only so that it can seize power. I cannot see what difference it makes to the working population whether the leading communists or the leading conservatives occupy the mansions of the town. The only revolution with a positive programme would be one to bring more freedom and happiness to every individual man and this, we know from experience, is precisely the aim to which communism is most hostile.

Mounier does not agree with either my views or the way I present them. In the course of a review he dismisses my article as superficial and childish. Nevertheless he is just as little prepared as I am to join the communist party; indeed among the left wing Christians he is one of the very few who, in 1944, did not join the National Front and was not taken in by any of the communist 'platforms'. But in spite of this all anti-communism, even when it is as mild as mine, makes him angry and suspicious. He is passionately eager for the revolution and he cannot see how it can possibly come about without the help of the vast communist machinery.

This is the tragic mistake so many progressive men make— particularly progressive Christians. In spite of Russian totalitarianism and the double dealing methods of the party, the working class—the only real revolutionaries—are sympathetic to communism however despicable they consider it. We can lay the blame for this situation variously at the door of Marxist agitation, of traitors in the administration, or of the complicity of the middle class and of the Church. But the fact remains that at present it is impossible to be actively anti-communist without also severing one's ties with the revolutionary element in the working class. And because progressive Christians are involved in this tangle they hate to hear communism criticised. Some of them, like Mounier, think the only solution to the problem is for the Christians to join with the communists to revolutionise the State and then, as soon as a socialist State is established, to Christianise communism. But the planners of this sort of campaign completely ignore the principles of communist ideology and its rigorous dogmatism which will not tolerate any compromise or accept any opposition or criticism from sources other than Marx or Lenin.

For my own part I am convinced that the only hope of revolutionising the world is in the hands of the working classes but at the same time I am equally convinced that such a revolution will only succeed if the workers break with communism. The longer this break is delayed the further the hope of revolution recedes. What good would a communist pseudo-revolution do? It would not liberate mankind from its slavery to the powers of production nor would it improve the social status of the workers.

17th October

In the course of my lectures to the surrounding towns I came across the story of one priest who from having been chaplain to the local Catholic Action group has left the Church and be-become a Protestant—and moreover is studying to be a Protestant minister. The Catholics of his town are deeply shocked and perturbed by the news but I can't help wondering whether the distress is not due, at least partly, to a suspicion, deep down in their hearts, that the trouble lies in the manner in which the 'true religion' is taught to the faithful. Both in catechism classes and in sermons it is always stressed that only the Catholic religion is true and a great many Catholics are convinced that an intelligent and honest person has no other alternative but to be a Catholic. The only reason they can see why not every-body is a Catholic is because either the non-Catholic brethren don't know the true religion or because they are not strong willed enough to do anything about it. Time and time again since my conversion my insistence that the majority of active communists act in 'good faith' has been met with scepticism or blank incredulity. Catholics do not fully realise, or tend to forget, that faith has also a personal value and that the heart plays a role in the act of faith. Of course it is true that faith is an act of the will—but we must realise how strong in the non-Catholic are the obscure and inexplicable driving forces of personal religious conviction.

How simple and straightforward everything would be for the Catholics of this town if only they could say that Father P. has left holy orders because he found it too difficult to cope with his priestly obligations or because he was infatuated with some woman. No doubt he would still have been ostracised among 'good Catholics' but they would have smiled indulgently at his 'human frailty' and the problem need not have troubled their consciences at all. But in this particular case nobody can throw mud at the Father's private life—it is unanimously acknowledged that it was exemplary and above reproach. He has not married since he left the Church and the Catholics are genuinely perplexed. I have tried to find out whether those who have mentioned the matter to me have any idea that they —both as individuals and a community—might be in some measure responsible for the apostasy of this remarkable priest. It is not impossible that the common practice of adjusting the gospel truth to their way of life, their self-centredness and their pharasaical formalism have ultimately discouraged him to the point where he finally broke away from his friends and the religion he had always lived and loved.

Of course in suggesting that the Catholics of the town should search their consciences I am not condoning the apostasy but I think the people might take a great step forward if they could understand the man and his motives. It seems to me tremendously important that Catholics should realise they form part of the social structure of the country because unless the majority do realise it—and act accordingly—the really fervent faithful, although they may remain within the Church will feel more and more out of sympathy with their co-religionists.

The story of Father P. reminds me of that of a young unhappy parish priest from a nearby diocese whom I knew in 1944. Poor in health, without sufficient means to support himself and convinced that his archbishop had no interest in his welfare he finally left the village with a young girl and married her. The pharisees of course washed their hands of the affair maintaining that it had been obvious from the start that he was destined for a bad end. I knew a good deal about this young priest and his struggles and conflicts. And I knew that the girl was by no means the cause of his running away. It was simply that she was on the spot when he felt he could bear things no longer. It is by no means the least part of the tragedy that the woman is so commonplace that even on the strictly human level he has not been able to make a success of his life.

1947

8th February

Jean, daughter of a musician and a talented performer herself, was in the YCW movement and later became a Franciscan tertiary. She had a longing for the state of perfection and each year she has grown less attached to her own will. When she realised that a perfect imitation of Christ was beyond her strength while living in the world she followed the advice of her director and applied for admission to the Poor Clares. The extreme poverty of the Order didn't frighten her at all because during her work in the Action groups she had seen far too much of the hopeless and unredeemed misery prevalent among the really poor. She was willing to consecrate her life for the purpose of praying and doing penance for the benefits of these outcasts of society. But when she entered the convent she was placed in the care of a novice mistress who told her to put away all thoughts of the world and its miseries and concentrate on attaining her own salvation and perfection. With the best will in the world Jean could not succeed. Ever since she had discovered Christ the only thing that mattered to her was to care either by prayer or by action for all those whom Christianity has never reached or who, because of a disgracefully unjust social structure have never learned that God loves them. Members of the YCW movement have little in common with religious narcissism as it is practised in many convents. After some weeks during which Jean tried her best to forget the world and take an interest in her own salvation she was in such a state of nervous tension that the good nuns feared she was 'possessed' and kindly but firmly dismissed her from the convent.

Today I was talking with a number of superiors of various Orders, and I was reminded of this case. They all complain that modern girls lack generosity, particularly those trained by Catholic Action groups. They attribute the steadily diminishing number of vocations to this lack of generosity. In some congregations the position is so serious that they are in danger of dying out. I tried to make them see that the lack of vocations might possibly be also partly due to the nuns' incomprehension of the modern Christian woman. These girls are not in the least afraid of the exacting work and the sacrifice which the service of God entails and they are quite willing to renounce the pleasures of the world. But they cannot accept particular styles of religious life; they are prepared to make sacrifices and obey their superiors but they do stipulate that both obedience and sacrifice should serve the kingdom of God and not be the consequence of masochism or sadism. The modern girl can find nothing admirable in Thérèse of Lisieux's going out on a cold winter's night to look for the Mother Superior's cat—and they refuse to imitate her. Equally they are extremely harsh in their condemnation of superiors who insist on this kind of obedience.

I told the nuns about Jean. Since she left the convent two years ago she has not plunged into worldly pleasures and amusements. Instead she lives in one of the poor quarters of Paris leading the truly heroic life of a missionary. Together with a few others including a teacher, a lawyer and a doctor, she is trying to bring Christ to the places where he is least known—the factories and the workers' living quarters. They earn their living as workers in the factories, shop girls, char-women—the only criterion is that work must be very low on the social ladder, must be poorly paid and enable them to live among the destitute. This self-inflicted poverty is no more desirable than that of the Poor Clares; in some ways it is less so because while the nuns, behind the convent walls are sheltered from much temptation and spared much knowledge of evil, the missionaries are in the middle of it and need both divine power and human force of character if they are to survive. But there is a growing number of girls—particularly from the YCW movement—eager to embrace this heroic vocation. Whilst many convents are short of vocations the Little Sisters of Charles de Foucauld can scarcely cope with all the applications they receive. Yet surely the rules and the heroism demanded by this vocation are at least as great as that of the more conventional Orders. The Little Sisters work in factories in the towns, tend sheep in the African desert, mend chairs among the gypsies; they live by the labour of their hands and this in spite of the fact that many of them have led sheltered and protected lives. A large number come from the upper classes of society and many have university degrees. I cannot help but admire them. If I had no other evidence of the active presence of the Holy Spirit in the Church, the existence of the Little Sisters would be sufficient to convince me of it. Yet they are by no means the only example of generously minded men and women grouped together to consecrate their lives to God. There are numbers of communities all over the country which live under similar conditions and deprive themselves of all comfort to try to share the miseries of the world—and they too have an abundance of vocations.

Not that I am trying to say the older Orders should copy the living and working habits of these new communities. They most probably have their own part to play; but in fairness to Almighty God they should at least investigate whether the shortage of vocations they suffer from is not due to failure to cater for the needs of the times. The Lord has promised that his Church will endure until the end of time but this is not necessarily true of institutions and congregations which were founded at a specific point in history to supply a particular period with the spiritual support it needed. They must either adapt themselves to the times or they must die. The Church and mankind will be no worse off for their disappearance because the Holy Spirit will bring new institutions into being to replace them.

15th March

A fairly large deputation of loyal and devout Catholics has

been to see the archbishop. The bulk of them were active working class Catholics who have only recently begun to live their religion. They complain that for months past they have been waiting for the parish priest to preach the gospel during Sunday Mass but each time he opens his mouth it is either to praise the Catholic schools and then ask for money for them or to encourage his congregation to use their vote 'well' in the coming election. It is hardly necessary to say that a good vote, in the priest's view, is one for the candidate who stands for 'order (which order?), private ownership (the workers have no property) and the support of family life' (no mention being made of the fact that the principal candidate for this party is known to be living in adultery). The archbishop both understands and shares their indignation and promises to write to the priest. One of the group however asks 'But if he listens to you as little as he listens to us doesn't our Christian duty demand that we shout him down in Church when he starts to talk politics instead of preaching the gospel?' This is rather a poser for the archbishop. However deeply he may personally sympathise with these Catholics who have the purity of the Church at heart he cannot possibly approve of a determination to transform the time-honoured sermon into a dialogue, or—worse—an argument. Of course in St Augustine's time at least at Hippo the congregation took a very lively part in the sermons, interrupting the preacher to ask questions or to object to what he said, but so much time has elapsed since then and the custom that only the clergy shall speak in the house of God has become so deep-rooted that it would take far more than the good will of an intelligent archbishop to dislodge it.

29th May

It really seems as though something is stirring in the Church. More and more of the faithful are beginning to realise that in comparing them to sheep our Lord did not intend them to be merely a bleating flock resigned to being slaughtered.

87

At the moment the public authorities are making fools of the homeless families. There is a rehousing committee in every town but instead of finding homes for the destitute it 'makes enquiries' and then records and files its findings 'for future reference' and nothing else happens. Yet there is no real shortage of accommodation. There are plenty of large houses which are practically empty—ten or more roomed flats occupied by a single old lady or a childless couple—and this while many destitute families are huddled in barracks which shelter them from neither cold nor rain. Some Catholics, remembering how concerned our Lord was during his lifetime with the lot of the poor and how he strove to help alleviate their misery, decided that they could no longer tolerate this state of affairs. And since the public authorities seem to lack the power to enforce the most elementary rules of justice they consider this duty falls to them to discharge. Today the newspapers are full of the story: during last night several empty houses were occupied by 'squatters' so that they can install there families whose living conditions are appalling. The press unanimously condemns this violation of the rights of private property—curiously enough even the communist paper is righteously indignant.

But the people responsible for this move have no doubts; they maintain that although the Popes have upheld the right of private property these rights must be kept in proper relation to one's duty to one's neighbour. According to Christian doctrine—as distinct from Roman law—an owner has no right to use or abuse his property as the mood takes him because he is only in charge of goods of which God himself is the owner. Although man has the right to make use of his goods for his own benefit he must also administer them in such a manner that they serve the common good of society. And since capitalist ownership refuses to acknowledge its social obligations the logical result is that it should be deprived of its rights.

Forty rooms — Three people

Seven people — Three rooms

Social injustice — Great Britain 1961

Social injustice — U.S.A. 1961

The squatters chose their victims very carefully to show they were not attached to any one party. The first building occupied belonged to a religious Order of teaching brothers— it is on the outskirts of the town and nowadays houses only a few sick and elderly brothers who not having understood that opening their doors to the homeless was a charge laid on them by Christ had to give way to the squatters acting on their behalf. The second building, a twelve-roomed flat of a former collaborationist which had been requisitioned by the communist deputy at the liberation, was seized by the squatters because the deputy rarely visited it, preferring to live in another flat in Paris. The third house they took possession of in the name of the homeless belongs to their chaplain's two old aunts.

Incidentally it is perhaps significant that the only priest in whom these shock-tactic Christians have full confidence belongs to one of the oldest aristocratic families of the district. He was brought up in Indo-China and when he was a small boy he once saw his father kick a coolie. He decided he must consecrate his life to the service of those his ancestors had humiliated. When he was ordained his bishop, recognising his outstanding intellectual gifts and knowing his family connections, wanted to put him in charge of a wealthy parish. The priest refused to accept it because he knew this was not the kind of work our Lord intended him to do. He began as a curate in the poorest parish of the town and it wasn't long before he was asked to be chaplain to the workers' movements of the diocese. Now despite his birth and his obvious nobility of bearing he is on the best of terms with and has the fullest confidence of the Christian workers who are only too ready to sneer at a priest in harmony with a world whose concepts the workers do not share and which, in their opinion, denies them the rights of existence.

11th June

The Catholic squatters continue to be in the news. Their

latest exploit was to lead a large crowd of homeless to the offices where their papers are held by the authorities. Using weapons looted from the days of guerilla warfare they threatened the head of the department and forced him to sign the papers. Then they marched to the headquarters and similarly forced the final formalities for the requisition of the 'occupied' property. It is unlikely that the authorities will accept signatures thus obtained but at least public opinion has been roused and there is hope that the official inertia has received a salutary jolt. It is ironical that the communist paper (voicing of course the views of the deputy) has called the squatters robbers, anarchists and gangsters. Several of them went to the paper's offices and told the editor that the workers take a very poor view of the paper's policy since it pretends to defend working class interests at all times. Another nice touch is that one of the squatters was a prominent resistance fighter and used to be an active member of the communist party.

16th June

There is in this diocese a religious association under the patronage of a great saint dedicated to the apostolate of marriage. Its members visit the houses of the very poor tracking down unmarried couples and those who only had a civil marriage ceremony. They take food and clothing to the people and try to get them to agree to having their marriage blessed by a priest. In this they are largely successful and can proudly point to the number of 'regularised conditions' they have been able to bring about. But the real results are not often as admirable as might appear. The couples often agree to be married in Church in order to please their benefactors without any notion of the deeper meaning of the sacrament of marriage and consequently with no intention of respecting its obligations. In fact very often after only a few months of 'married' life they apply for a divorce. The situation is particularly tragic if, as I have seen happen in more than one case, one of the partners concerned has started to practise their religion.

After the divorce such people have an almost insuperable problem—they cannot remarry yet they have neither the vocation to a single life nor a wish for celibacy. I can't help feeling that the pious ladies and gentlemen of the association might do better to distribute their alms without any strings attached.

25th June

During a short journey a few days ago I bumped into a man I had known before the war. He is a kind of modern Benedict Labre. In 1933 he left the navy as a captain to become a Dominican but rapidly discovered that God did not intend him for a student and apostle to the intellectual world. So he directed his steps to La Trappe and like Charles de Foucauld tended the pigs and there he stayed for two years. But for him as for P. de Foucauld La Trappe was only a stage on the road to his true vocation which turned out to be that of a pilgrim. After leaving the monastery he wandered from one place of pilgrimage to another, from Lourdes to La Salette, Pont-Martin to Sainte-Odile always on foot begging his food as he went or working for a few days on a farm. He joined the army of professional tramps, sleeping with them in barns and under hedges, sharing his bread with them and always telling them how good God is even to the poorest of the poor. The call up in 1939 found him in the south of France where he had the utmost difficulty in getting to see the port-admiral. In his rags and tatters he didn't look exactly like a naval captain. In 1945 he was demobilised with the rank of Vice-Admiral and could hardly wait to take up his pilgrimages once more. The world, even the 'Christian world' sees only the folly of such vocations; it is convinced that an admiral could do much more 'useful' work at his post as an officer rather than by leading the kind of life X leads. But am I wrong in believing that today more than ever it is imperative that the dynamic power of shocking and causing commotion must be restored to the message of Christ? It is terrible that the religion of Christ should have become so

91

orthodox that it no longer surprises and that Christ's followers can hardly be distinguished from those who do not believe in him.

9th October

By chance today, on yet another journey, I found myself in a place where I thought I remembered the Little Sisters of the Poor ran a home for the aged and where a friend of mine came after she had made her profession. She was the daughter of a wealthy business man and three years ago, when I knew her, one of the leading lights of the town's social life. She was passionately in love with life and its pleasures and she collected wordly successes with the same avidity that others collect stamps. But shrewd observers noticed that from time to time in the middle of a dance or a conversation her glance would wander as if she were looking at some horizon and only her body remained in the room. Then one day came the news that she entered the Little Sisters of the Poor. No one knew why—there was no hint of a secret love affair or that her social success was finished. I found her just as she was about to dress the feet of a cantankerous old man who never stopped grumbling and insulting her. The girl who had always been so elegantly turned out was now clad in an old piece of rough material— not that even that could entirely rob her of her charm. Her face showed the marks of an ascetic life but her eyes shone even more than formerly. They reflected a deep peace and an extraordinary joy such as is not of this world. I didn't need to be told that she is supremely happy.

Yet humanly speaking there is nothing sadder than a home for old people. Physically and mentally deficient children usually have some sort of charm and for them there is a faint hope of improvement and restored health. But these old people have often ended up in the home after a life of disillusionment and frustration. They are usually surly and quite often downright spiteful and vicious. An infinite measure of love is needed as well as the patience of a saint if one is to care for them

92

without becoming bitter and discouraged. The Mother Superior assured me that my friend is making a wonderful thing of her vocation.

1948

1st February

During this last year the progressive elements of the Church in France have suffered a persistent campaign of denunciation and calumny. According to reports the Holy Office is being inundated with letters from France claiming that Catholicism in this country is in 'mortal danger'. Some priests are accused of being 'in league with heretics and tending towards schism' because, worried by the gulf and incomprehension which divides Christendom they try to understand the Protestant and Orthodox points of view. According to the 'dogmatists' it is almost a repudiation of the Church's authority to admit that the separated brethren do not bear the whole responsibility for the breach in the visible unity of the Church and that the behaviour of a great many Catholics—even Church leaders— accounts for the unfavourable idea so many people have of the Church. It seems that some people no longer regard it as sufficient to accept that the Holy Father is the successor and heir of Peter and that his decrees in the matters of faith and morals are infallible. The dogmatists would have us regard every one of the Pope's pronouncements, every point of view uttered by him or one of his Cardinals on any subject, as directly inspired by the Holy Ghost. And as for the ecumenical movement that is, *a priori*, considered highly suspect.

Because many Catholic theologians and philosophers think it important that the revealed truth should be re-thought in the light of modern discoveries and mentality they are accused of furthering religious relativism and breaking with tradition. Yet the Lateran Council decided that Christian revelation does not depend on any one philosophy or even on a particular theology. People forget that some of the greatest doctors of the early Church sought and found the intellectual framework of their faith in the philosophy of Plato and that St Thomas and the scholastics, much to the indignation of the 'dogmatists' of their time, broke with a thousand-year-old tradition by adopting the philosophy of Aristotle. But it seems that what St Thomas was allowed to get away with has not been tolerated since.

It reminds me of a wonderful sermon I heard at Toulouse in praise of St Thomas and how some Dominican fathers who were present were annoyed because the preacher had described St Thomas as the 'greatest theologian of the midlde ages'. According to the fathers the priest ought to have described him as the greatest 'theologian, philosopher and scholar of all times'. Nor, apparently, did they have any idea how intellectually dishonest such a statement would have been.

For my part I have never been able to understand why people should hold the view that after one given moment in history Christian thinking should be reduced to repeating and learning by heart the formulas laid down the masters of the thirteenth century or, at best, to commenting on them. Why should not a Catholic be at liberty to consider existentialism or Bergsonian concepts. From the natural standpoint can one maintain that Aristotle was more Christian than Blondel or Bergson?

Because a group of artists attempt to break with the Christian pseudo-art so popular in the devotional shops in St Sulpice, they are accused of secularising the saints; the dogmatists even demand that these modern paintings should be removed from the churches.

Because a few priest workers and some intellectuals among the chaplains and members of the YCW movements are somewhat impressed by the apparent revolutionary efficacy of Marxism the dogmatists accuse all Catholic Action movements and all priests connected with them of making common cause with atheist communism.

There is no end to the dogmatists' grievances against anyone

94

they regard as 'progressive'. What amazes me most is to discover the type of people who subscribe to the dogmatist wave in France. Thanks to friends in high places I was allowed to see some of the denunciatory letters to Rome and to my astonishment I found some from eminent members of a religious house prominent in the south of France. Apparently during all the years of their studies these men have had it drilled into their heads that truth is inseparable from Thomism and that by going off the beaten track of Thomism one must necessarily also deviate from Christ and the Church. No wonder that with the best of faith they denounce the 'deviationists'. But at least their dogmatism is limited to the realms of philosophy and theology; the signature I found of a priest who is well known in artistic circles in Paris and often mentioned in the sensational newspapers literally made me gasp. I don't need to be a psychoanalyst to see the connection between this priest's 'dogmatism' and his everyday behaviour which is anything but 'dogmatic'.

Of course I was not surprised to find that a particularly large contingent of the 'informers' comes from a class of people who read certain types of periodical which claim to have a monopoly of Catholic thought or newspapers which pretend to defend 'God's cause'—without mentioning that the 'cause' in question is mostly that of a world which is Christian only in name. These dogmatists by no means limit themselves to upholding theological integrity. Theologians, philosophers, sociologists, scholars, artists, worker priests are all named as part of a monstrous plot against the Church and against 'Christian civilisation'. In the background the bloody hand of communism is said to be visible pulling the strings.

But most stubborn of all among the dogmatists are well meaning laypeople who under the pretext of defending the Christian family denounce and calumniate their brethren in Christ who are so unfortunate as not to share their concept of the Christian faith. In a small journal they spread the worst type of political-religious confusion.

5th March

An important ecclesiastical dignitary, fearing that the dogmatist agitation may have regrettable consequences for Catholic life in modern France has invited a few of them to meet some of those whom they denounce. We, the latter, tried in vain to drive it home that we are perfectly entitled to adhere to such and such a theology, philosophy, scientific theory, political doctrine or artistic concept, and that we, on our side, would never have dreamt of doubting their sincerity or the authenticity of their faith just because we did not agree with their ideas. The only thing we ask is that they in their turn should respect our liberty and leave us to live and express our faith according to our convictions. One monk felt that he put the whole problem in a nutshell by quoting Aristotle's *Amicus Plato, magis amica veritas*.

11th April

A few days ago I was invited to give a lecture on communism in a poor parish on the outskirts of Paris. The church is a modest building and the presbytery in no way differs from the poorest dwellings of the district. Three priests live there in a little community. Each takes his turn at working in a factory in order to earn the money they need. They have realised that today even more than in St Paul's time it is essential for the servant of God to live on his earnings if he does not want to be labelled a 'stooge of capitalism' or a sponger even if, in reality, he is starving because he cannot both fulfil his ministry and earn enough to live on.

The door of this community house—the term presbytery would sound odd to the ears of this working class population—is always open and the people can come and go as they please. If they arrive at meal times they can sit down at the table and share the meal and they can all see that the parish priests have no better food than the poorest working class families. These are the types of things that matter so much because, like Thomas, most people will only believe what they have seen with their own eyes and touched with their hands. The priests have no beds. In the evening each of them unfolds his mattress, which during the day is stored in a box room, and gets into his sleeping bag. As there are more mattresses than priests there is always room for a visitor on his way through the parish and I was invited to spend the night with them.

What is the apostolic value of such a life? I wasn't there long enough to be able to discover statistics about the work of this team of genuinely evangelical priests but what I did see was that they really take part in the life of the district. People call them by their Christian names and no one would dream of treating them with that exaggerated deference which people often affect when speaking to priests. Problems regarding relations between clergy and laity do not exist in this parish—it goes without saying there is only the state school. The communist head teacher is a great friend of the priests. We had our meal with him and during my talk he sat in the front row. They are all on friendly terms with each other and such details are more important in these working class districts than most people imagine.

Next morning when I left I thought that Pope Pius XI must have great pleasure as he watches these priests from his place in heaven. It was he who declared that the most unforgivable crime the Catholics of the nineteenth century perpetrated was to drive a deep wedge between the Church and the working class. In the parish I have just left that wedge has vanished; the Church is at home in the very midst of the workers.

Last night I gave a lecture in yet another parish on the outskirts of Paris and again I was the guest of the parish priest. What a contrast. Here we are surrounded by the stately mansions of the upper classes. Outside the hall where I lectured there were dozens of gleaming cars and inside many costly furs. And the difference between the living conditions of the priests in charge of the parishes is just as striking.

The priest here lives with his niece in a lovely two-storey

house with thick carpets and expensive looking furniture. The dishes are solid silver and the food is exquisite. Also the priest is only available for those who have an appointment with him. I am not intending to condemn my host. I am convinced that he sincerely loves our Lord and does everything in his power to serve him as best he can. Nor has he acquired wealth in the course of his life as a priest because I noticed his family arms on the silver ware and that is probably where the carpets and furniture come from; nor do the parishioners criticise the presbytery in any way—it is in keeping with the district.

Yet this parish is only four or five miles away from the other one and the inhabitants of the poor parish can hardly be ignorant of the fact that by no means all priests live like their own—and as far as they are concerned it is the priest of the wealthy district who corresponds to their idea of the traditional parish priest. They almost certainly don't accuse their own priests of hypocrisy or ulterior motives because they have first hand experience of the religious fervour of these men. But the admiration they have for their own priests does not extend to the Church as a whole.

On more than one occasion I have seen this tragic conflict at first hand. People love and admire the missionary priests who are poor and live among them but at the same time they know that these are only volunteers in the army of the Church which, on the whole, always remains 'middle class'. People conclude that, like the world, the Church consists of rich and poor and that the poor priests live with the people while the rich priests remain with the exploiters. They do not believe that the Church is one family of equals because they have never seen proof of it. If only those in charge of the Church's future will realise that modern men and women will no longer be swayed by Sunday sermons. They only accept demonstrable fact.

5th May

Judging from the way people speak of France as 'the eldest daughter of the Church' and talk about 'Catholic and French for ever' one would imagine that France is wholly Catholic. Statistics show that thirty-five out of the forty million Frenchmen are officially Catholic. If only this were so in reality. Of course the official return of scarcely ten per cent of the adult population practising their faith is not realistic either since among the non-practising there are many who consider themselves Catholic however vaguely. They insist on their children being baptised, on being married in church and above all on having a Catholic funeral. For many of them it is no doubt something in the nature of an insurance policy but since one doesn't take out an insurance unless one is reasonably convinced of the ability of the company to protect one it is permissible to include these people among the Catholics. Yet I wonder if the Church authorities really realise how large a percentage of French Catholics hazard the Christian truth in this way.

During one of my lecture tours in a strongly Catholic district, I met Professor J., an active and intelligent socialist with a real democratic tradition behind him who thought he found in me a kindred spirit. We took to each other at once and I was invited to spend the week-end at his house. He is not totally ignorant of Catholic tradition because he was baptised as a child and attended catechism classes. His wife, on the other hand, who also lectures, knows as much about Christianity as she knows about the religions of ancient Egypt and China—or rather she knows less about Christianity than she does about the ancient religions because for one reason and another she has read fairly extensively about *them* whereas since her family were Freemasons she has always regarded Christianity as malignant without ever enquiring into its message. I don't mean that she is naturally intolerant because in fact she is kind and sensitive and gets on with almost everybody. Indeed it is her tolerance which makes her so hostile to Catholicism which, in her opinion, is the last stronghold of feudal mentality, of the Inquisition and the witch-hunt.

Naturally their children have not been baptised and in fact although they live very close to the cathedral I am the first priest they have ever spoken to. I can see in the children's faces how surprised they are to see me eating, drinking and smoking like an ordinary human being. They are even more surprised to learn that I am not at all in favour of capitalism, that I admire the same artists and writers as they do and that I am not opposed to state schools.

I can't help wondering what kind of impression this family has got from their first contact with a priest. For my part I am glad to have made their acquaintance; something tells me they will prove good friends.

The whole family came to see me off at the station and on the way we met quite a number of people who had attended my lecture, most of them apparently dumbfounded to see me in the company of the Professor who is considered in the district to be a fanatical enemy of the Church. Probably some of them expect to hear shortly of his conversion—others of mine!

16th October

Never did I suspect that the Church employs 'beadles'. I know from bitter experience that many people do not shrink from acting as informers to the Church authorities—and incidentally I have discovered that the majority of bishops are neither proud of them nor in any way encourage them to watch over the words and movements of any priest. But official 'beadles' . . .

I have always been on filial terms with my ecclesiastical superiors and my archbishop has treated me with much more kindness than my own father ever showed me. He has been generous and understanding even to the point of witholding a stern rebuke when, from an objective point of view, I certainly deserved it. He reproached me but all the time I felt that far from being complacent about it he suffered as parents always suffer when they must punish their children. But how wrong I was to imagine it was the same everywhere.

I understand that amongst all the priests in this large town hardly one has ever been in personal contact with his archbishop. They can only manage to get to the prelates of diocesan administration who have neither the grace nor apparently the gift of spiritual fatherhood. I am told that it couldn't be otherwise in this vast city with its numerous parishes and the constant demands on the archbishop's time. I know very little about it; perhaps I am naive in my concept of the successor of the apostles as primarily a pastor of souls appointed to spread the gospel—but I cannot think of any gospel precept requiring his attendance at countless ceremonies and fashionable receptions.

Today a young priest came to see me in terrible distress. He had been summoned to the archbishop's palace because some tale bearer had accused him of taking liberties with regard to certain liturgical and pseudo-apostolic traditions. He tried to explain to the prelate on duty that his parishioners knew nothing of origin of these traditions and that he felt it his duty as a priest to interpret the message of Christ in a way they would find comprehensible. He could have saved his breath. The official was only concerned with the law; to him, apparently, souls and their salvation were only abstract concepts. The young priest felt as if he were facing a police officer who was reprimanding him for having broken the regulations.

I couldn't help sympathising and sharing his indignation because I have always had a horror of this type of official—I have found them to follow the same pattern whether the state they served was democratic, totalitarian or communist. Personal difficulties or problems of conscience did not exist as far as they were concerned—the only thing that mattered was the law or, as the case may be, the regulations. It is very distressing to think that such bureaucrats should also exist within the Church.

17th October

Last night I was telling a·priest friend this story and how

indignant I was about the high-handed behaviour of the particular prelate in question. My friend who knows many of the clergy in high office tried to make me see that the Church, being a visible society, must also have an administration and that, regrettable as it may be, good administrators are rarely also men of great spiritual and apostolic gifts. He also assured me that, out of office, the prelate in question is an extremely holy and charitable priest but that being in charge of what I can only call the archepiscopal police force it is difficult, if not impossible, to act differently without neglecting his duty towards canon law and the diocesan regulations.

I am prepared to admit in theory that the priest's arguments are valid but nevertheless the whole process repels me. I think I should have been more at ease in a Christian community similar to those of the first centuries. Also I would prefer to hear the Church described as a visible community rather than a society because the very term society implies an administration and a police force.

12th December

The other day a group of young priests were debating whether a social revolution could possibly benefit the Church which has become weighted down in the course of the centuries by its own administrative apparatus. Registers, archives and enquiries take up far too much of the clergy's time. A certain young archbishop whom I happen to know well and who received his appointment immediately after the liberation began his career by declaring that he was not going to be the administrator of the diocese and that instead of playing the role ecclesiastically equivalent to that of chief constable he was going to be the leader of an active apostolate. He took an enthusiastic interest in the work of his priests but it wasn't long before he had to admit defeat in the face of pressing secular engagements. Today his time, like that of most of his colleagues, is absorbed in an interminable round of activities, blessing bells and statues, presiding at ceremonies, opening this and that, being present at official gatherings and, worse, administering his diocese. The same thing is true of the young priest—the most unorthodox minded, as soon as he is put in charge of a parish, must devote a great deal of his time to the routine of administration. Incidentally today we even speak of 'administering' the sacraments.

None of the priests taking part in the discussion were either communist or pro-communist. And they all know that a revolution on the communist pattern which is practically the only kind of revolution feasible nowadays, would inevitably bring in its wake untold misery and suffering to the people and would destroy many human values. Moreover it would test men's moral resistance, and particularly that of Christians, so severely that many would succumb to the pressure. So it is impossible to wish that such a revolution should really take place.

But just what is the alternative? How can the Church extricate herself from these false traditions which prevent her true spirit from reaching the masses of the people and may even be responsible eventually for her total exclusion from the new 'world' which is being formed? During the pontificate of Pius XI there was some hope that the Church might shake off the dust of the centuries by her own efforts and might once again represent the world of tomorrow as she led the way when first she was founded. But the history of the last fifteen years might well lead one to believe that such hope was mere fantasy.

My friends maintain that a revolution would destroy the Roman curia, the diocesan and the parish administrations. They admit that such a revolution would also—at least for some time—cripple every attempt to spread the Christian message but they believe that the prospect emerging after the collapse of communism would be truly wonderful and that at that moment the Christian message could be presented to the world in its true and pure form and nobody would dream of accusing the Church of being the accomplice of reactionaries.

Such a vision is of course utopian although undoubtedly an administrative and orthodox Church provides communism with more platforms for attack than a purely evangelical Church would do. The reason why I have set out this problem at such length is because the preoccupation of these priests seems to be a symptom of the deep perplexity which prevails in the minds of some of the Church's most loyal sons.

1949 — 51

1949

14th March

I have just returned from a lecture tour in the west of France which lasted several weeks and gave me the opportunity to see for myself at close quarters the religious set-up of a district renowned for its Catholicism. The people were extremely hospitable and had I accepted all the proffered invitations I might have been sure of board and lodging for some considerable time. But I had a feeling that there was more glitter than gold and soon tired of festivities.

Here, as in other Catholic districts I have visited, the parish priests amazed me by their authoritarian attitude. Some of them are very concerned with the great problems facing the Church and her effect on the modern world but more spend their time and energy passionately arguing against the appointment of lay-teachers in the schools and running down those appointed.

Yesterday one of these teachers came to see me and told me how difficult the situation in her village was because of the priest's hostility towards the state school. The three classes are housed in three separate buildings. My visitor is a practising Catholic and a former YCW. She told me that one of her two colleagues is a Protestant without any strong sectarian prejudice and the other does not practise any religion but is interested in the problems of our faith and would welcome an opportunity to know more about it. Since there is no private school in the parish there can be no question of rivalry but that doesn't deter the parish priest from devoting two sermons out of three to attacks on the 'godless' school and frightening the parents by telling them of the terrible risks their children run by being in constant contact with those impious people, the teachers. Naturally the teachers take exception to this and the result is an atmosphere which poisons the whole life of the community. Without mentioning that I had spoken to anyone in the village I tried to persuade the parish priest that it was wrong of him to live in a state of constant warfare with the local teachers. I suggested that perhaps it would be better for everyone if he, who by vocation must be interested in the children's education, could work in harmony with those sharing that interest. I could have saved my trouble—I might have been talking Chinese so involved is he in his 'task' of waging war on the teachers.

I wonder if this attitude isn't linked with the fact that he seems to lack the courage to preach the exigencies of Christian charity to his extremely materially minded parishioners. It may be that in attacking the teachers the poor priest is giving vent to his suppressed aggressiveness without being rebuked. But at the same time neither the Church nor the children profit by this state of affairs.

18th March

Of course it would be ridiculous to maintain that the priests are always to blame for strained relations between Church and school. I have known teachers whose anti-clericalism was at least as bitter and as senseless as the clericalism of the priests. But yesterday I learned that a priest who is really aware of his mission to spread peace and harmony wherever he goes can sometimes effect surprising changes in the customs of the countryside.

I went to a parish where a few years ago the relations between priest and teachers could not have been worse. The priest missed no opportunity to complain of the misdeeds of the 'atheist' school and the teachers took their revenge in history lessons when they talked about the reactionary character of the Catholic religion and ridiculed the beliefs and devotions of the older generation. Although the school adjoined the presbytery the inhabitants were not on speaking terms. If the priest asked the children to assist at a funeral or a baptism the teachers arranged the lessons so that the children were not free to go to

Church. Quarrels about the times of catechism classes and the dates for solemn Holy Communion were an integral part of the gossip of the neighbourhood. The villagers themselves were divided into two camps, those following the priest and those siding with the teachers. At election time they voted not so much for a political programme as for the candidate favoured by the priest or the teachers respectively.

But three years ago a new curate came to the village. On his first day after having introduced himself to the mayor he paid a visit to his neighbours the school-teachers. His reception was hardly encouraging but he took no notice and visited the school at regular and frequent intervals either to make enquiries about a particular child or a social function or in order to ask for the sort of help which neighbours can hardly refuse each other.

Before long the spiritual atmosphere of the village had changed completely. Quarrels were forgotten and the veiled hostilities ceased. True the teachers have not been converted to the faith nor has the priest relinquished his convictions, but their relations, from being those of good neighbours, have become really friendly. Often the priest is invited to dinner at the school and the teachers do for him all the little jobs so much appreciated by a single man. They exchange books and spend the long winter evenings listening to records together and discussing their joint problems and in this way the only three cultured people in the village make life more pleasant for each other.

The days when the children had no time to attend the choir or the catechism classes are gone. This is all fixed by mutual agreement and the priest himself goes to ask for the children's attendance at ceremonies. But most important the priest can nowadays really preach the gospel, that is he can encourage love instead of hatred, and the enmity between the two 'camps' is gradually dying out because they have lost their leaders.

25th March

A certain young and brilliant doctor of medicine, a gifted heckler, has attended most of my lectures in this district. He passionately, at times violently, contests the truth of the picture I draw of conditions in Russia. Actually I have no difficulty in swaying the audience in my favour since I have lived in Russia and he has never been near. His heckling has contributed greatly to the success of my lectures. In this district where the population is traditionally very conservative in its outlook I don't think the average Catholic shares any of my feelings for communism. While I attack it because of its atheism and the practical consequences of its contempt for the dignity of the individual I am not under the delusion that the wealthy land-owners whom I notice at my lectures particularly respect human dignity in their relations, for instance, with their farm-hands. The reason they are so afraid of communism is because its doctrine of equality fundamentally threatens the preservation of their wealth and privilege and threatens to raise their farm-hands to their own social level. My doctor is the black sheep amongst the orthodox population of the region and the fact that he opposes me so violently immediately places me on the 'right side' in these people's minds. Against my will I am becoming the defender of 'order and property'. In fact I am much more akin in every respect, except the apologia of the communist party, with the doctor than I am with them. He is a fervent Catholic who played an active part in the resistance during the war and like so many others he thinks it will be impossible to rejuvenate the Church without a revolution to make a clean sweep of all privileges and habits which stand in the way of the progress of mankind. Like so many others he sees in communism the ideal revolutionary power and consequently he has dismissed from his mind all the objections against communism until the day when the revolution shall have triumphed. Afterwards, he argues, one would find a way to safeguard the intrinsic liberty of

Christianity and supply the faith with new fields of action.

In Paris or Marseilles his ideas would not be particularly original but it is very different here where the Catholics almost unanimously equate the kingdom of God with the established order. The doctor is therefore ostracised by his co-religionists; no priest visits him and the bigots in their usual repellant manner belittle him by casting slurs on his private life. Some of them are not above trying to set his wife and family against him.

I went to see him at his house where he told me all this with a sort of wry smile. So far he has managed to stand up to it but I couldn't help feeling he is nearly at the end of his tether and I shouldn't be surprised to hear shortly that he has left the Church and joined the communists. Of course the 'righteous' will rub their hands and say how right they were to mistrust him. It probably won't even occur to them that they themselves could possibly have any responsibility for the apostasy of this Catholic.

When I was talking to some of the more tolerant local priests I tried not to justify, but to explain, the doctor's attitude. It is certainly tragic that a prominent Catholic should become a follower of communism—yet how many prominent Catholics are avowed capitalists and shamelessly profiting by a socially unjust order? Yet they are not cold shouldered by the Christian society or ignored by the priests—on the contrary they occupy the places of honour in the Catholic movements and the charitable institutions. Just why do Catholics behave so differently in the case of this doctor? If his political opinions make a sinner of him why not treat him as other sinners are treated—with charity. The way his case is judged as an exceptional one cannot fail to confirm the impression many people have that the Church subscribes to two different moral standards and that its behaviour is conditioned by political considerations.

4th October

Four months ago I came here, to Morocco, as the editor of a

Catholic paper. I should be terribly disappointed if the paper turned into a 'family bulletin for the Catholic ghetto' in this Moslem country. Somehow I must get the Moslems to read it and it must make its contribution towards a better understanding between the 'faithful' in Morocco each of whom profess one of the great monotheistic religions, i.e. Mohammedanism, Judaism or Christianity.

What gave the most painful shock when I arrived last May was to find how inconceivably ignorant the local Christians are in all matters concerning the eight million Moslems. I approached priests who have lived here for twenty, thirty and sometimes forty years and asked them for information about Moslem customs and beliefs. Apart from silly anecdotes they had nothing worthwhile to tell me. I was told that the Moslems are fanatical and intolerant, that they have only contempt for the 'Romans' and the 'Nazarenes' and I was surfeited with stories about their polygamy and their loose morals etc. A few people did mention the courage Moslems show when they are not ashamed to kneel in the street and public parks at the hours of the ritual prayers. Yet no one that I questioned had taken the trouble to make an intelligent study of Islam as, for instance, the White Fathers have done in Tunisia. I myself knew precious little about it all when I came and that little was based on the few books I had read by Massignon, Father Abd-el-Jalil and Dermenghem. But nobody I spoke to had read anything at all on these lines.

Considering the example the clergy give it is hardly surprising that the Christians in general are so ill informed. They live in this Moslem country in a self-inflicted, ghetto-like isolation, organising ceremonies and running charitable organisation in exactly the same way as if they were in Brittany or Alsace or any district in France.

There are however a few exceptions. Some days ago I met a group of Christians in Casablanca whose entire spiritual life is geared to the problem of how to communicate with the

Moslems. They make a serious study of the Koran and the local Moslem customs and they pray for understanding and love for the faithful followers of the Prophet. But there are few Christians in Morocco who do so. So many of them speak of the Moslems as if they were pagans, completely ignoring the fact that they, too, are spiritual descendants of Abraham.

I feel that the explanation for this indifference of the Christians towards the Moslems must lie in the 'conqueror complex' under which many of them still labour. No one has ever taken the trouble to tell them that such a complex is diametrically opposed to the Christianity they profess. They seem to think that they are superior to the Moslems because their army has conquered Morocco. Their 'charity' disposes them favourably towards the scheme of permitting the Moroccans to profit from the achievements of French civilisation and to be received into the Church of Christ provided they have the intelligence to apply, but it is beyond their comprehension that the Moroccans might have something to teach them or that Islam could make a positive contribution to their faith.

As for the clergy, they came here as chaplains to the French army. Gradually they extended their ministry to the colonists but there are very few among them who realise that they could also be missionaries of the faith. A young and very devout priest told me quite seriously the other day: 'My superiors have sent me here to minister to the French people and the others are not my concern'.

I gather that, fortunately, this state of affairs is gradually changing. The bishop is said to be deeply disturbed by this ghetto-like attitude and some of the younger clergy have set themselves the task of making amends for the errors and omissions of the past.

Under the conditions prevailing at present any missionary action with a view to converting the Moslems to Christianity is doomed to failure. I don't mean to say that I believe the

Moslems to be completely impervious to the Christian message
—that would be tantamount to saying that the Christian
religion is not universal—but I am convinced that in the eyes
of the Moroccans (and also in those of most other Moslems)
the Christian religion is too much the religion of a colonially-
minded Europe. To become a Christian would to a Moslem
mean consenting to foreign domination.

Needless to say I know nothing about God's plan for
Morocco but judging from purely human experience and
psychological knowledge the conversion of Morocco to
Christianity is impossible as long as the colonial regime lasts.
Its very existence fosters inferiority complexes and resentment.
But this does not dispense the Christians and the clergy from
their missionary task. It would have to be based of course on its
members living a truly Christian life perhaps on the lines of
Charles de Foucauld. Incidentally this is the avowed belief
of those Christians I mentioned earlier who are concerned for
the Moslems.

1st November

Today for the first time I had the honour of meeting Father
Peyriguère. I had of course heard a great deal about him but he
himself far surpasses his reputation. He was born, raised and
ordained in Bordeaux and in 1928 he went to live among a
Berber tribe in the foothills of the Atlas mountains. Following
the advice of St Paul and the example of Charles de Foucauld
he was determined to live as a Berber among Berbers. He has
succeeded so well that, apart from the Sacred Heart sewn on
his tunic, he cannot be distinguished from the rest of the
tribe. Sometimes when a couple have lived together for many
years they grow to be so like each other in features that they
could be taken for brother and sister and the same thing applies
to Father Peyriguère; he looks so like a Berber that tourists
often regard him as a typical representative of the people.

Many Moslems spoke to me about him with great reverence
and apparently he is regarded as a *marabout* (holy man) through-

out the whole region. People travel for days on donkeys or camels to spend a night near his hermitage and sleep with their head on the stones he has walked on—an action which is supposed to draw down God's blessing on the sleeper.

How has he managed to overcome the innate mistrust and fear of everything alien in a people famous for its passionate adherence to its peculiarities? During the first years of his missionary work he was probably accepted because of the medical care he gave them in a spirit of unselfish dedication. And also he begged from the resources of his French and Moroccan friends and thus saved the lives of many of the poorest members of the tribe. But a great many other monks have done the same without achieving anything like Fr Peyriguère's high reputation.

It seems that his main distinction in the Berbers' eyes is his fierce independence in dealing with the official administration. His worst enemy couldn't accuse him of being a government agent because his fine sense of independence and his courage have led him always to stand by the tribe and its interests— whenever it seems to him that the authorities are acting un- justly or inflicting undue hardship. The Berbers are more in need of justice than alms.

Incidentally the problem is nowadays more or less the same everywhere. What a pity it is that the ecclesiastical heirarchy has not yet grasped that in the modern world the Church will not impress the hearts of the people with the message of Christ by organising schools and distributing free meals. The temporal world is quite capable of meeting these needs of education and national assistance. Only by placing herself in the vanguard of the army fighting for social justice and peace against atom bombs and other atrocities will the Church make the people of this century aware of the 'depths of the riches' of divine love. Organised Christianity is still wearing its medieval dress and has not yet been adjusted to the miseries of the modern world.

9th November

In my capacity as the editor of a paper I am asked to a number of cocktail parties and other fashionable activities and I can't help enjoying them. I have been separated for a very long time from the 'fashionable world' and to mix with it is exciting, particularly as I adapt myself easily—perhaps too easily—to any situation and environment. In a shorter time than I would have believed possible I have learned to join in the 'brilliant'—and futile—conversation which is *de rigeur* at this type of gathering. It is only when I get home that I begin to feel disgusted with myself and a sense of humiliation.

Last night I was a guest at an 'ultra-distinguished' party. The 'intellectual élite' of Casablanca was represented by some of its more glamorous members (in my opinion a rather over-rated glamour) and the fashionable ladies vied with each other in the attempt to parade their culture and their spiritual preoccupations. One of them, a glass in one hand and a caviare sandwich in the other, approached me and murmured 'Reverend Father, I have often wondered why God allowed temptation to enter the world. Surely if we were not tempted we could not sin and the world would be better all round.'

At the best of times I don't like religious and philosophical discussion in the garish surroundings of cocktail bars because it always seems to me to drag the whole thing down. The woman who addressed me wasn't in search of truth but was merely trying to be clever so I replied, with a perfectly straight face—'But Madam, that is obvious. God permitted temptation to enter the world so that you should have the pleasure of succumbing to it.'

Did she understand what I meant to convey to her? I doubt it but in any case I don't think she will feel like submitting her 'scruples of conscience' to me again. The role of fashionable priest doesn't seem to me worth the effort. If I stay in fashionable circles it will be out of curiosity and not because I admire the people who haunt them.

11th December

A young man, a fervent Catholic and father of a large family came to see me today. Until his marriage he lived a completely chaste life and since his marriage he has scrupulously observed the laws of the Church concerning Christian marriage with the result that his wife has had seven children in eight years and that her health has broken down. The problem which this family faces is not an academic one but a question of life and death. The choice can best be summed up thus: either the couple continue to conform to the regulation of the Church thereby making it a near-certainty that within a short time the seven children will be orphans or, if they want their children to grow up under the loving care of their mother the couple will have to refrain from receiving the sacraments—and to such fervent believers as they are that is unthinkable. Of course it has been recommended that they should live as 'brother and sister'—they have tried it but the temptation was so strong that the husband was almost driven to adultery. And of course there are the 'methods' of limiting conception whose use is authorised by the Church but in this particular case they have had no effect.

Now if it were not that I am confronted with this particular case I would not raise the question: a law can be perfectly justified even if its application proves almost impossible in special cases. But the fact is that the *majority* of Catholic families labour under the same difficulties. Must the divine commandment 'increase and multiply' be applied in the same rigorous sense as in the Old Testament and the times of the Patriarchs? In those days the world was empty and a large family ensured the power and wealth of the patriarch, but things are vastly different in our days of city-dwellers when the danger of over-population is more real than that of under-population. Since the Christian Church has suppressed polygamy—authorised by the Old Testament—and has discontinued circumcision—another law adopted by the same

authority—could it not make an effort to adapt its sexual morality to the new conditions in which mankind lives? I am fully
aware of how delicate the ground is which I tread. The Church
is much more amenable to modern ideas in the matters of
dogma and interpretation of Holy Scripture than in matters
of sexual morality. None the less I think that many priests who
are concerned with the spiritual welfare of the people con-
fiding in them would in their inmost hearts agree with me.
But unfortunately there is little we can do towards changing
the present outlook except to hope that the hierarchy will find
out for themselves how grave the problem is.

1950

5th February

Dr D. is not a religious man in the usual sense of the word
but nevertheless he is very interested in spiritual matters and
respects the faith of others although as far as he is concerned
it is the problem of religion as such which occupies his mind.
During an international congress which he attended in Rome
he had two weeks in which to study the Rome of Christians at
close range. He took every opportunity to see and learn as much
as possible and the Holy Year with its numerous ceremonies
intrigued him.

Like many visitors to Rome he was shocked to see how the
Vatican clings to old traditions and how much unprofitable
wealth is stored up in the basilicas and other churches. How
could this remind one of the humble and poor Christ of the
gospel? It was no use my pointing out that the Holy Father
himself lives an extremely simple life. He is quite prepared to
believe that the Pope's life is an austere one and that he doesn't
profit from the riches of the Vatican but that doesn't make
matters any better. 'Why' he says 'is so much wealth permitted
to lie idle when there is so much misery in the world?' Christians of the middle ages took it for granted that the individual

religious's vow of poverty could exist side by side with the enormous wealth and magnificence of the religious houses. Dr D. however, and the majority of modern 'pagan' men and women see this as sheer hypocrisy or maybe even greed. Are they altogether wrong? Did not the Popes themselves in their social encyclicals teach that the goods of this earth are primarily destined to satisfy the needs of mankind? Christian teachers of moral philosophy agree that private property lying idle may be appropriated if it can be proved essential to the needs of others; incidentally this is one of the classical arguments used in favour of the policy of colonising undeveloped lands. Dr. D. argues—what is the good of all these riches lying dormant in the sacristies and safes of the Vatican when the sense of the human solidarity is stronger today than perhaps ever before. The crowns of gold and precious stones adorning the statues of the saints are far more likely to provoke indignation than admiration and piety.

Are the ecclesiastical authorities really aware of this trend? A return of the Church towards the simplicity and poverty of the first centuries might do more to spread the gospel in the modern world than all the pilgrimages and processions and perhaps even more than the miracles of Lourdes and Fatima.

6th February

For some time now I have been involved in arguments about the question of the Church's concept of its duty of evangelical poverty. Last night I went to dinner with a prominent industrialist, a devout Catholic who gives much of his time to parish affairs. He expressed his own—and other people's—astonishment at the grand style in which the parish priest lives. Apparently no business magnate can boast of such an ornate and luxurious office. The furniture is solid oak, there is a fitted cocktail bar with varied and expensive drinks, the priest has a large American car and so on. But the most incredible part of the story is that the priest in question is a Franciscan, a spiritual son of the Poverello.

I must confess that when I came to Morocco I was myself startled to see the comfort in which the majority of Franciscans in this country live. I had imagined (my knowledge of Franciscans being only second-hand and influenced by the *Fioretti* and the various lives of St Francis I had read) that the Franciscan Fathers who are the main bulk of the clergy in Morocco would be inclined to make it a point of honour to lead a deliberately simple life to make an impact on both the Moslems and the colonists whose only ambition is to amass material wealth. I was soon disillusioned. Of course some of them *do* live very sparely indeed and St Francis must feel proud of them, but the majority are so ostentatious in their luxury that even the richest Parisian parishes could not compete. And in addition these sons of St Francis refuse to preach the gospel to the poor. Since the Order is short of vocations they cannot fulfil all the parochial needs in the country and have had to relinquish a certain number of parishes to the Salesian Fathers, Sons of Charity and secular priests. One might have expected that they would have retained the simple, poor parishes and given up the wealthy ones but in fact the opposite is the case. The Franciscans have monopolised the ministry of the well-to-do. And as neither their spiritual nor their intellectual training has prepared them for this type of ministry the results are little short of tragic. Blinded by the glitter of society life and the polite manners of their flock they fail to preach the hard reality of the gospel teaching. Instead they are so flattered to be admitted to 'nice' circles that throwing their own judgment overboard they adopt class prejudices and defend class privilege. Thus there is the ironic spectacle of Franciscan Fathers as the most fervent defenders of the colonial regime and definitely hostile towards the movement for the emancipation of the Moroccan people.

11th March

When I became a Catholic and first visited monasteries and convents I was always struck by the simplicity and purity of heart of the inhabitants. Watching austere Benedictines laughing and joking like so many children during their daily recreation made me see what our Lord meant when he admonished his disciples to become as little children.

Nor is this child-like spirit only to be found in the monasteries. When I was teaching I often noticed that the Catholic students were more cheerful than the others and thoroughly enjoyed games and songs which to the others meant nothing at all. It was possible to pick out the non-Catholics by their seriousness. I don't mean the Catholics didn't take life seriously but it was obvious that the temporary problems and momentary vexations were not nearly so important to them as to the non-Catholics. They were in a sense detached and carefree even while deeply involved in the typical troubles of their age and the anxieties of their world.

But this childlike simplicity must not be confused with childishness. The distinction has been borne in on me very clearly this last year when I have had my meals with a dozen or so monks. The conversation hardly ever rose above teenage level. They had no understanding of the world's problems and the Church's present apostolic task made hardly any impression on their minds. The continual joking was not only childish and banal but disheartening. Every time a visitor to the town is invited to be Monsignor's guest I can see how embarrassed he is by his religious brothers' silly talk.

23rd May

I have made one of the parish priests furiously angry by organising and presiding at two lectures by Jean Herbert which dealt respectively with *Yoga and Christianity* and *The Contribution of Hinduism to the World of Tomorrow*. A large audience listened attentively to the scholarly account of this man who amongst all modern Frenchmen has made the closest study of Hindu spirituality.

He is a Catholic and although a great admirer of Hinduism has never renounced his own faith. But his familiarity with the concepts of other religions evidently makes him reluctant to adopt the childish pride which Christians display when they naively believe themselves to be the only ones in possession of any divine truth—a pride which often leads them to treat the Hindus and Moslems like so many idolators. Jean Herbert insists that the Hindu religion not only leads millions of men to a close union with God but that we Christians can learn much from Hinduism. He is not, of course, advocating that we turn Hindu but he does think to know more about Hinduism might help us to lead a fuller Christian life. He said: 'Unless a world-wide disaster overtakes us and destroys the human achievements of centuries it seems inevitable that, unlike the world of yesterday, the future world will no longer be divided into a great many watertight compartments keeping peoples totally ignorant of each other. The future culture and mode of life could unite the elements of all the riches acquired and preserved by various present day groups and this union could lift us to a hitherto unknown high level of awareness.'

These and similar statements led to the outburst to which the priest I referred to treated me after the lecture in the presence of a large audience. 'Are you not ashamed of yourself' he shouted 'to take the chair at a lecture where it is said that rays of human enlightenment will shine from the banks of the Ganges and not from those of the Tiber?' Of course Jean Herbert did not say anything of the kind—he is not preaching a kind of composite religion. But no theologian has ever dared maintain that there is no authentic religious value outside Christianity, nor that the latter is in actual possession of the whole of religious truth, so why should we not be able to profit from the religious experience of Hinduism? They of course can learn much by enriching their spirituality in the light of the gospel truth and the Christian mystical and ascetical tradition. The early Fathers found inspiration in the Jewish Bible and in the mysteries of oriental religions and neo-Platonism without in the least imparing the uniqueness of the Christian claim.

I am always rather at a loss when confronted with Christians like the priest in question. If I hadn't been trained in psychology I might interpret their intolerance as being simply the expression of their great love for our Lord and try to explain that loyalty to Christ does not entail sectarian mentality. I could remind them of St Justin, the philosopher martyr of the second century who fervently loved and admired the work of the divine Word whether he came across it in philosophy or poetry, in Greek or Roman sculpture. Why should we be afraid to admit that the Holy Spirit can be seen at work in Hindus and Moslems? But my experience of the human unconscious mind has led me to believe that intolerance is usually nothing but a compensation for weak faith. Because a person is not too sure of their faith they refuse to acknowledge truth elsewhere. Knowing this I find it impossible to blame the Christians for their intolerance. After all it is natural that they should cling to their faith. Of course one wishes it were so strong that it didn't need the kind of protection given to the feeble and the childish. But that is a different problem. Curing disease involves far more than recognising the symptoms.

Often I surprise and even shock people by my enthusiastic sympathy with Hinduism or Islam. Yet far from alienating me from the Christian religion this sympathy and enthusiasm confirm my love for it. I cannot understand why Christians should worry about the historical discoveries of the nineteenth century which revealed the resemblances between dogma and ceremonies in the Christian religion and the beliefs and cultural practices of other religions. Probably it is because generally we are not sufficiently aware that the facts on which the Christian religion is based are unique in the religious history of mankind.

20th August

F., a professor of French literature, has been coming to me for instruction prior to being received into the Church. He is an extremely intelligent man and has realised that Christianity is

123

the door leading to human freedom and the only means by which humanity can be saved from the onslaught of totalitarian and materialistic forces. Gradually he also came to see the fundamentally supernatural character of Christ's teachings and then he asked to be baptised. His mother is Jewish and his father officially a Protestant but both of them are really atheists. They brought up their sons to believe in reason, science and progress. F. has not renounced either reason, science or progress but he has seen their limitations and it is the Christian faith which offers him the longed for perfection. An hour ago he came into my office and, dropping a small booklet on the desk, said with an air of bewildered sadness: 'You will understand that after seeing this I cannot possibly go on with my conversion'. One glance at the ominous booklet told me that it was the encyclical *Humani Generis* of Pope Pius XII. F. feels that in this document the Pope is condemning as near heresies everything which he, F., has for years held dear and which has brought him to the threshold of the Church. He feels that the encyclical justifies all the grievances his father and others have against the medieval obscurantist practices of the Church.

How could I put his mind at ease? I explained that the encyclical contains no explicit condemnation and was issued as a safeguard against heresies for which certain intellectual groups of Catholics might fall and I emphasised the distinction between an encyclical and the definition of a dogma. But even while I was speaking I knew that my words lacked the necessary conviction because I know only too well that had *Humani Generis* been published before I had become a Catholic I should have felt exactly the same.

During the pontificate of Pius XI and the first years of his successor's reign it seemed as if the Church had boldly taken its stand in the progressive camp. The social encyclicals, Catholic Action, the new missionary ideas, the renewal of biblical and theological studies, the kindness with which Christian democrats were treated at the Vatican, the encouragement given to progressive writers and thinkers all seemed to indicate a Church policy which had severed its ties with the world of yesterday and was concerned to go with the world of tomorrow. It was noticeable, and we rejoiced, that in France and Germany at least the bishops were chosen from the ranks of priests known for their 'advanced' ideas. Of course diehard anticlericals obstinately refused to believe that the Church was no longer the bulwark for the protection of reactionary and conservative ideas; they insisted that her 'pretended progressiveness' was part of a campaign and they pointed out that the Pope had blessed General Franco's and Mussolini's armies. But it was relatively easy to discredit these grievances. The extraordinary vitality of French Catholicism and its direct turn to the 'left' soon persuaded unbiased people that, without deliberate ill faith, one could not justifiably accuse the Church of subscribing to conservatism. The welcome which the popular front party gave to the Papal Legate gave rise to the hope that even the traditional enemies of Catholicism might be prepared to bury the hatchet and to admit that the Church was marching with the new world. The immediate consequence of this new spirit was a flood of converts to Catholicism among the intellectuals. And when, after the liberation some bishops who had been known to collaborate with the Germans were removed from office and replaced by men in favour of the new ideas and one of the most 'advanced' bishops was raised to the rank of Cardinal, everyone thought that the Vatican had 'got the idea'.

But from 1946 onwards there were rumours that the reviews *Esprit* and *Témoinage Chrétien*, both very progressive, were to be placed on the censured list. People who professed to know what was happening in Rome said that the ageing Pope was listening more and more to the counsels of a kind of coalition formed from all sorts of reactionary groups. The communist successes in France and Italy, the difficulties the Church was experiencing in the countries behind the iron curtain all added weight to the arguments the 'dogmatists' used against those who favoured a break with tradition. The fear of the communist danger was a pretext for suspecting not only politically left Christians but philosophers, theologians, scholars, economists, promoters of liturgical reform, advocates of the ecumenical movement, in short all who in one way or another seemed inclined to favour breaking with routine and orthodox methods. All were arraigned as accomplices of communism. The accusation was so blatantly false that we found it hard to believe the dogmatists could be taken seriously.

The first really ominous signs appeared on the horizon when in the course of a purifying action aimed at the very centre of intellectual life, several leading teachers of theological revival were banned from teaching and dispersed to small towns. Obviously—and the victims were conscious of it—these measures had been taken so that the full force of the Vatican's wrath should not fall on the heads of men who were the pride and glory of their Order in the modern world. Knowing all this it was no surprise to me when *Humani Generis* was published.

So I wasn't really astonished when F. refused to be baptised. No doubt this will scandalise the pharisees who will loudly proclaim that one does not become a Catholic because one is attracted by a certain type of philosophy or theology, still less by a particular political trend, but because one believes in Jesus Christ. No one in their senses would deny that—but we are not pure spirits. Human beings, in order to grasp even the purest of spiritual truths, must be helped by a psychological process to interpret it in terms comprehensible to the individual mind. Obviously nobody who already belongs to the Church would be justified or could be excused if he were to break with her even if she changed her course entirely with regard to contemporary events, but I can understand and sympathise with a catechumen who under the circumstances cannot accept his baptism.

Certainly if I, at the moment when my interest in Catholicism was roused, had been confronted with bigots and dogmatists instead of meeting, as I had the good fortune to, Christians in the forefront of the struggle to bring Christ to our times, the divine grace most probably would not have triumphed over all the objections my mind would have made.

25th September

For the last month or so the dogmatists have been much in the news. I am told that F.'s case is far from being an isolated one, that very few intellectuals are being instructed in the faith and that many of those who were on the threshold of the Church have stepped back.

According to news from Rome the Holy Father is surprised and deeply grieved at the reactions to his recent encyclical. It is being reported that the text originally submitted to him was much more explicit in its censure and that he refused to sign it because he insisted it must be merely a solemn warning without anyone feeling it was aimed particularly at him and that above all it must not be capable of exploitation for partisan ends. Incidentally Pius XII has several times pleaded for moderation when people have attempted to interpret his teachings too severely. I have read and re-read *Humani Generis*. It seems to me more than likely that the Holy Father was not aware of the very definite aims the people who prepared it must have had in mind. All the same anyone acquainted with the history of the Church in France today could almost head every paragraph with the name of one or the other of the most prominent leaders of the movement for religious revival in our country. It seems rather a large coincidence that the wording of the encyclical should lend itself so particularly well to the odious use the dogmatists make of it. And of course I am hardly impartial since the censured thinkers are precisely those whom I had chosen for my leaders because, it seemed to me, they were the most faithful interpreters of the gospel and its spirit.

The encyclical frowns upon those Catholics—theologians, philosophers and scholars—who 'fearing to be suspected of turning a blind eye to the discoveries made by science in this era of progress, endeavour to ignore the teachings of the Supreme Pontiff and thus are in danger not only of putting an undue distance between themselves and the revealed truth but also of encouraging others to commit the same error'. The danger is by no means imaginary but the warning should not only be addressed to those who commit the error. If the religious leaders would restrict their pronouncements to subjects on which they are competent Catholics would listen to them with respect. But as the hierarchy attempts to touch on every conceivable subject, from football to veterinary practices, from space travel to midwifery, many people are inclined to pay no attention to their observations even when they are speaking about sacraments and morals. Nothing harms authority more than the abuse of authoritarian practices.

26th September

Never since I first became a Catholic have I had the slightest difficulty in believing the dogmas of the faith. Yet I have always tried to express them in terms other than those used by the scholastics. I am fully aware that the rationalism of Aristotle and St Thomas has long satisfied the needs of Christians who sought to understand their faith and no doubt still satisfies many today. Nevertheless I found that for me personally and for many educated people to whom I had to bring the message of Christ, this philosophy is utterly alien. Either we must try to understand and express the revealed facts in concepts familiar to us (and no one would urge this more than St Thomas) or we must be resigned to accepting the faith of the 'man in the street'.

I remember learning about an ecumenical council which solemnly defined that the Christian revelation is not fixed to one particular philosophical, scientific or theological system. Is that any less true today? God forbid that I should scorn the faith of 'the man in the street' or even scorn the manner in which it is usually taught. All I want to emphasise is that this method, as far as educated non-Catholics are concerned, is more likely to obscure the truth than to reveal it.

27th September

The dogmatists accuse some theologians of 'irenical'[1] leanings. This sin is supposed to consist in an acknowledgment that the Christians separated from Rome are not entirely wrong and that, to bring about a reunion of Christendom, the Church will also have to acknowledge its errors. It is all too obvious that this attack is aimed at one Dominican Father in particular who advocates the reunion of all Christians and recently wrote a book which was severely censured by Rome.

This Father C. has spent his whole life trying to pull down the dividing walls which prejudice and ignorance have erected between the various Christian creeds and he told me one day:

'If we want to find the root of the evil separating all Christians we must look for it in Rome. We can mostly agree on the dogmas, the primacy of the Pope could be recognised by the separated Christians provided that it is understood rather on a democratic than on a totalitarian basis, but the trouble comes with the ecclesiastical administration which is too faithful a copy of the temporal government of empires. Indeed one would have to be completely ignorant of Church history if one were to believe that a Patriarch of Antioch or Constantinople, whose churches are apostolically founded, could agree to receive his orders from the Monsignori of the Roman congregations. As it is I am always somewhat surprised to find the bishops of the Latin Church accept them the way they do.'

The 'irenists' have never doubted a single dogma of the faith but in memory of our Lord's wish that we should 'be one as the Father and I are one' they treat Protestant and Orthodox Christians as brothers instead of sitting in judgment on them.

[1] St Irenaeus, *ca* AD 130, was called the Peace Maker for his efforts to reunite separated Christians to the fold.

Consequently they know much more about them than the average Catholic does and they realise that very rarely does one find a Christian separated from Rome who is a heretic in the true sense of the word as it is understood in Catholic theology. Is it then not largely our, the Catholics, fault if they still remain outside the visible ecclesiastical unity? Do we, according to the wishes of our Lord, reflect the Church of Christ in such a manner that every man of goodwill is able to recognise it?

If we are to criticise the 'irenists' must we shape our relations with the Protestants on the pattern set by the intolerant Archbishop of Seville?

2nd October

Apparently I have done a grave wrong to his Holiness Pius XII; my friends and I have too readily succumbed to the fear the present Pope welcomes the dogmatists' campaign.

A bishop in whom I have every reason to trust has just returned from his *ad limina* visit to the Holy Father. He received a warm welcome and the Pope showed deep insight into and understanding of the apostolic preoccupations of the progressive Catholics. He told the bishop that he was heart-broken at the manner in which certain people abused his encyclicals and he repeated that he had never intended to censure the bold seekers of truth. The bishop was particularly impressed by the Holy Father's eminently supernatural spirit. He said 'It is inconceivable that the Pope should allow any other motive to prompt him than that dictated by his conception of his very special mission'.

This bishop had ample opportunity, on the other hand, to notice that by contrast those who surround the Holy Father are far from being in the same serenely supernatural frame of mind. Political intrigue abounds particularly since there is mortal fear, more human than Christian, of communism. The *Monsignori* are reputed to favour the dogmatists because they increase confusion between two factions, one which is trying to drive a wedge between the faith and an out-of-date civilisation and the other which tries to keep a sense of proportion in the face of communist empty promises.

According to the bishop, if the dogmatists want to obtain the Pope's approval for certain measures they label those who refuse to identify pseudo-traditions with Tradition as being enemies trying to undermine the purity of the faith—and it is only too easy to pick out clumsy efforts of some over-zealous innovators. To sum up the bishop categorically denied that the Holy Father is prejudiced one way or the other but he saw a powerful dogmatic group hard at work in the Vatican. I am terribly pleased at this news because nothing is harder for a believing Catholic than to feel himself at variance with the Supreme Pontiff even in matters not directly connected with the faith.

28th December

I had hoped to find my Parisian friends in a calmer frame of mind than I am after this latest apparent triumph for the dogmatist group. But they were not. Some of them have lost courage because they think the gulf between Christianity and the modern world is widening. They all confirm—what I already knew—that conversions among intellectuals in France are almost non-existent. Some have rebelled and feel that a break with the Church is inevitable. Nearly all my priest friends are in disgrace, at least unofficially, and all have been relieved of their teaching posts. Several religious have been sent away from Paris to remote houses of their Order. One, who until recently was very 'progressive' has joined the dogmatist camp; it is hard to believe that it is a genuine change of opinion rather than the move of an opportunist. I think if I had not had the inspiration to look up Fr T. I should have returned to Morocco even more depressed than when I left it a week ago. But this good Father, although the encyclical directly attacks his views and makes him the black sheep *par excellence* in the eyes of the dogmatists, is quite unperturbed. He was very amused to find that I attached so much importance to the apparent victory of the dogmatists and attributed my despondency to my extreme 'youth'. He himself is convinced that mankind is only on the threshold of maturity and not yet done with its growing pains. He maintains men are just like teen-agers who think they are adults. Like all children they attach undue importance to events which, years hence will only be straws in the wind. 'We are only amongst the first Christians,' he maintains, 'and yet we imagine that we have arrived at the fulness of time. This, incidentally, is nothing new—even in St Paul's day the Christians thought the second coming of our Lord and the end of the world was at hand. In the course of the Church's history the same thing has happened again and again. The Seventh Day Adventists were not inaugurating anything when they declared the Second Coming would take place on a fixed date (each time further removed). Our brethren of the faith will probably have an indulgent smile in the year A.D. 100,000 when they read in their history books that we worried over some encyclical or some "dogmatist" victory. Just think of the passionate debates of the Byzantine theologians as to the sex of angels or, in the Middle Ages, the discussions on the distinction between *efficacious* and *sufficient* grace. How remote it all seems to us now.'

The Father's optimistic (because universalist) way of regarding history boosted my morale considerably. I am ashamed that I let myself be depressed to such an extent by what seems to be an indication that the ecclesiastical hierarchy is making a new start. I am all the more surprised at myself because I have always adhered to Hegel's thesis, which tallies with that of the good Father even if from a very different point of view, that all history is incomprehensible when seen at too close a range or from one particular angle. History only makes sense in so far as it is universal.

The trouble with me was that at the time of my conversion I was too enthusiastic about the 'progressive' turn the Church was taking under Pius XI and, like others, I find it somewhat difficult to feel at ease in—what seems to be—the Roman new look. I fully agree with the Father's view that it is absurd to attach too much importance to the rising wave of dogmatism—but what am I to do while I wait for another wave to supersede this one? If I were a layman I could temporarily withdraw from Church activities and concentrate on an active temporal life, restricting my religious ambitions to practising the faith according to the law. But being a priest it seems difficult to retreat in such a manner.

It would not be so bad if I were the only priest in this sort of confusion but unfortunately many find themselves in the same dilemma. During the few days I had in Paris I did not meet a single priest who could say he felt at ease with present Church policy. One of them, a brilliant figure in the intellectual circles of Paris, has publicly broken with the Church. He plans to found a new Christian community following the lines of the gospel and tradition. Of course this is not new either and I cannot believe that such an enterprise, while it lasts, can do anything except add to the confusion.

1951

10th January

I asked Joseph Folliet to come to Morocco and give a series of lectures on social topics. He cannot be said to be 'progressive' in the sense of making common cause with communism but he is a man of great courage and noble spirit and certainly the best interpreter of the Church's official social doctrine—which is why I invited him. The majority of Catholics in Morocco neither know nor understand the famous social encyclicals.

But Folliet's lectures did not make the impact we had hoped. In none of the six towns in which they were held did they have any real success. Certainly prominent Catholics turned up but all too obviously they only came to fulfil a social obligation. They listened with the same respect with which one listens to the Sunday sermon but drew no personal conclusions from the lectures. And the ordinary Catholics were conspicuous by their absence. Yet lectures are very popular over here and explorers, authors (even minor ones) can be sure of talking to big audiences. I am certain that had Folliet talked about, for instance, folk songs, on which he is an expert, or even on a purely spiritual subject, the halls would have been full. But social subjects interest only a small minority.

I have been discussing this with some of my friends—why the French in Morocco should be so indifferent towards social problems. We decided it was most probably an unconscious fear. The most humble of them realise they enjoy a number of privileges which generally are independent of their personal merits. The ordinary white people—let alone the commercial and colonial magnates—are very arrogant about their 'racial superiority'. Women who in France did all their own chores over here can afford to employ servants. I can see every day at the printing works how the 'European' workers instead of contributing to the traditional workers' solidarity, often treat their native workmates quite harshly and as if they were inferior.

Only a small minority among the Christian population are aware of their missionary duties in this Moslem country and make an effort to put into practice the social demands of their faith. The others, meaning the broad mass, although they are not 'evil' and generally treat their workers less harshly and their servants more humanely than non-Christians, still rigorously restrict their charity to individual cases and refuse to acknowledge their general social obligations. Most of them are convinced that Arabs are morally inferior and must be kept in a state of subordination. In other words they think of themselves as 'good masters'. In order to preserve their peace of conscience they refuse to become interested in social problems and particularly in the social doctrines of the Church. If one listened to lectures by people like Folliet and felt the obligation to acknowledge one's social duty to the people of Morocco life would become extremely complicated. Better ignore him!

The majority of Christians, however, are quite sincere in so far as they do not knowingly wish to act against the moral principles of the faith. I have so often witnessed their difficulties with regard to problems like morals in married life that I know, that in their hearts, they realise that life in Morocco would lose much of its charm if they were to listen to instructions dealing with the Christian doctrine in social and colonial matters. The parish priests avoid broaching the subject and leave well alone.

25th January

For the last fortnight I have been on a lecture tour in Algeria. In some ways the situation there is similar to that in Morocco, in others quite different.

As soon as one crosses the border one senses being in a different country. In spite of everything the spirit of Lyautey is still alive in Morocco—the colonists generally adapt their buildings to the local style and except for two or three churches they harmonise with the surroundings. The Algerian colonists on the other hand seem to insist on keeping aloof from the natives and, expressing this in their buildings, they have as far as possible faithfully copied their French villages, building houses in red brick or grey slate with pointed roofs and the church and town hall 'exactly as in France'. In spite of the scorching sun the priests wear their black cassocks (in Morocco they generally wear white or khaki). And racial segregation is far more stringent than in Morocco.

But above all the French in Algeria are firmly convinced that their methods of colonisation are unsurpassed; many really good Christians said to me: 'If the natives of Morocco are agitating for independence it is only because France has not destroyed every illusion of Morocco's ever becoming independent. Here in Algeria the scheme of assimilation has been successful because the Algerians, after being encouraged to study, are proud to be regarded as fully fledged Frenchmen and do not want independence.' Nearly all the Frenchmen whom I spoke to attributed the agitation of the nationalist Algerian leaders to personal ambition and refused to take them really seriously.

But the few conversations I had with the Algerian Moslems convinced me they by no means share the colonists' views on the benefits of assimilation. Granted a number of them are proud to be French citizens but all they profit from that honour are the rights and privileges attaching to that status. As for being accepted as truly equal the French have no intention of permitting it—and I can't help thinking that before long these 'French Algerian' Moslems, if they continue to be frustrated in the hopes the policy of assimilation has awakened, will start a much fiercer war against colonialism than the type of attack we might see in Morocco or Tunisia.

And the number of nationalist Algerians is far larger than the colonists realise. True Algeria has never yet been a united state or a nation but the French make a great mistake in relying so much on past history. Even in such a short time it was quite obvious to me that Algerians are wakening to national consciousness precisely because they have gradually become familiar with French culture and customs.

The Christians of Algeria seem to be even less interested in missionary tasks than their brothers in Morocco, although the Algerian population is predominantly Moslem. Of course individuals and many of the White Fathers do splendid work but the deliberate ignorance of the majority of the faithful and the average clergy in matters of Islam is truly appalling. The daily life of the Church is conducted exactly as if they all lived in some part of France.

11th March

Amongst the European population of Morocco the percentage calling themselves Catholic is much higher than the percentage of practising Catholics in Paris but religious fervour is not very great. Catholic Action is practically non-existent and as I have several times mentioned I can find no evidence of the missionary spirit. On the other hand as in Italy, Spain and the other Mediterranean countries, processions and the various liturgical manifestations are much favoured. Nearly all the churches are too small, at least on holidays and also I have to admit that the Catholics of Morocco give generously to the Church—the annual subscription to the Church funds amounts to considerably more than in the most Catholic metropolitan dioceses. The result is that the clergy here live very comfortably indeed and grants in aid of the construction of churches are truly outstanding.

But it does seem that religion as such hasn't much to do with the loyalty the French of Morocco apparently show for the Church. It is more a question of imitating, consciously or unconsciously, the native mentality which is very strong in a country like Morocco where the Sultan is both the temporal sovereign and the highest religious authority. Islam does not distinguish clearly between the temporal and the spiritual spheres. More often than not it happens that the 'enlightened' Moslems are complete atheists—but they still call and consider themselves Moslems. They don't believe in the religious dogmas of Islam and they don't practise its ritual but they acknowledge the Sultan as the principal link between the Moslem nations. The majority of Frenchmen in Morocco seem to regard their ties with the Catholic Church in much the same way. Thus when funds were collected for the construction of the grand 'cathedral' of Casablanca the most effective catchword was always: 'Casablanca must have a cathedral worthy of France!'— and it worked wonders.

The Moslems do not differentiate between the European settlers. For them they are either *Romans* (in memory of ancient days) or *Nazarenes*. The Europeans accept this state of affairs and frequently one hears someone being called a

Christian who believes neither in the Holy Trinity nor in the Incarnation. One is a Christian because one is French.

Beside the authorities set the example. Since time immemorial the majority of high officials have been Freemasons because Morocco has always been one of the principal fiefs of the 'brotherhood'. On the other hand countless official religious ceremonies take place from which not a single Freemason would choose to stay away. The Governors set great store by the bishop's presence at the Protectorate's official ceremonies and all public manifestations. The bishop, however much he would like to keep away from these fashionable functions finds that he must attend because his predecessors did so in their eagerness to play the role assigned to them by worldly authorities. Nobody, not even the majority of the clergy, seems to conceive that the Church in Morocco could have any other mission than that of giving colonialism her moral support.

In editing my paper I have taken care never to appear to favour colonialism. When it was first published I was highly amused to watch the general surprise of people to find a Catholic paper criticising the French authorities and branding as social injustice the treatment dealt out to the native workers. It was beyond their comprehension. I have had letters by the score pointing out the harm *Maroc-Monde* is doing to French prestige, which needless to say is sacred and must not be criticised. The public reaction is as vehement as if I had criticised the heroism of the soldiers of Verdun in a speech commemorating the battle.

One of my fellow editors conducted an impartial enquiry into the scandal of high rents and speculation in flats in Casablanca. Recently at a meeting of the paper's administrative council which the bishop attended, a prominent Catholic personality, an underwriter and president of innumerable 'charitable' organisations, spoke with tears in his eyes about the sacrilege the paper had committed against France. Not even the bishop could convince these gentlemen how imperative it was that in a Catholic paper justice should take precedence of the perpetual gratification of patriotic vanity.

The Moslems wondered at first whether the apparent refusal of *Maroc-Monde*, and of the bishop, to make common cause with colonialism, was not merely a clever ruse but they are just beginning to realise that their categories of *Roman* and *Nazarene* may not always be accurate.

21st May

This state within a state—French Morocco—is in the throes of an election campaign. The 'third electoral assembly', i.e. the representatives of 'other interests' at the governing council must replace half its members. Although the governing council is purely consultative it tries hard to create the impression of being a minor parliament. Its members have no specific political role but they are capable of exerting considerable influence in the various administrative departments of the Protectorate and thus of rendering valuable service to their electors. That is why so many candidates are entered for each constituency.

One would assume that the majority of Christians in Morocco are fairly wealthy but in fact the opposite is true. They are mainly minor civil servants, small tradesmen, clerical or manual workers, free lance journalists etc. Politically speaking however the Catholics form the extreme right wing. Countless retired Colonels living in Rabat, Rez, Oudjda etc. preside over the parish councils—and retired colonels are seldom progressive.

In Casablanca, where almost a third of the French and Catholic population live, a small group of a dozen or so important business men have always spoken on behalf of the Catholics. They preside at the advisory committee for the building of new churches, speak on behalf of the Catholics at all the official and private functions and generally advise their co-religionists in electoral matters.

I am told that during previous elections posters inviting

Catholics to vote for the 'proper candidate' were even fixed
to the church doors and that a fair number of priests preached
the election campaign from the pulpit. Yet the 'proper candidate' was by no means always a pillar of the Church. Often
he was of dubious character, a small business man, divorced
and remarried, whose only merit was that politically he was
known to be extremely right wing. When one knows that the
Church refuses to administer Holy Communion to divorced
people and regards them as public sinners it is surely nonsense
to accord such men power in the political field.

As soon as the election campaign started I received visits
from numerous prominent Catholics who invited me to their
houses. In fact they wanted to convince me that it was essential
to use the paper as a means of propaganda for the 'proper'
candidate. Although the bishop has ordered his priests not to
participate in the election campaign I, as the editor of a
paper, am in a different position. Therefore on principle I
agreed to join in but the difficulty came when I had to decide
which, among all the names presented, were the 'proper'
ones.

It was agreed that the Catholics should be invited to vote for
the 'French influence in Morocco' patronised by the radical
party. But when I found out that one of the candidates they
proposed to support was a freemason and four or five times
divorced and remarried I put my foot down and categorically
refused to play.

The result was open war. One industrialist who used to
support the paper by paying for several dozen subscriptions
has just notified me that he will do nothing more to help me.
Others who used to advertise refuse to receive our representative. A band of hooligans has been commissioned to make
trouble at my lectures and I am being violently attacked in the
columns of one of the daily papers. Whereas up till now
people were apparently interested in my communist past
they suddenly have begun to condemn me for it and to in-

sinuate that since I refuse to toe the line I probably never broke with the communists.

The bishop was pressed hard to declare himself in favour of the candidates chosen by my opponents. He flatly refused to do so but the day before the election a pamphlet was distributed in all the parishes of Casablanca and printed in all the papers (except *Maroc Monde*) signed by prominent business people known for their religious 'convictions'. The pamphlet was very cleverly devised in so far as it insinuated—without actually saying so—that Catholics should vote for the masonic candidate with the full approval of the bishop. As it was circulated at the very last moment a protest was impossible and the Catholics, like the sheep they are, voted *en masse* for the recommended man gaining him a huge majority. All I could do was to publish, through *La Croix* in Paris a violent protest against the Machiavellism of the Catholics of Casablanca.

30th June

I don't think that all the people (among whom are some very good Catholics) who maintain that the Church must support a reactionary policy have necessarily only their class interests at heart. They almost certainly believe that the Church herself is vitally concerned with and responsible for a certain social order and that by defending their own class interests they also work for the kingdom of Christ. Nothing else could explain their violent antagonism when I refused to comply with their wishes.

A dozen prominent business men took the time and trouble to go to Rabat to see the bishop and ask him to relieve me of my post as editor of *Maroc Monde*. When they saw he had no intention of giving in to them they threw caution to the wind and said bluntly: 'Either you dismiss him or else you will not receive the sum of sixty-five million francs we had decided to put at your disposal for the building of churches'. From the psychological point of view it was the worst possible move and the bishop, very naturally, replied: 'Even if I had intended to dismiss him your threat forces me to abandon any such plan. Do you really think a bishop can be bought—even for sixty-five million francs?'

The bishop, himself an honest and upright man not familiar with the world of business, was extremely surprised to find that the 'delegation' were men who, before this, had been regarded as my friends and had frequently asked me to their homes. I did my best to explain to him that however 'gentle-manly' a capitalist might be in private life he is a vastly different person where 'business' is concerned.

15th July

The clashes following the Casablanca elections have after all done some good. Quite a number of Catholics, including university men and ordinary workers and even some business men, are indignant that a small ultra-reactionary group should claim the right to speak on behalf of all the Catholics of Casablanca. They decided to form a group and in their turn send a delegation to the bishop. This gave him the opportunity to declare publicly that no individual or group has the right to speak on behalf of the Church.

11th December

One of the things I have learned since I came to know the Christian world which never ceases to surprise me, is the wickedness—often unconscious—of many pious people. Non-practising Catholics have often said to me: 'I don't go to Church but I consider myself a better Christian that those who do: at least I don't speak ill of other people'. In its absolute form this statement is obviously false because there are untold numbers of daily communicants who never speak ill of any-body; moreover the non-practising Catholics are far too prone to pat themselves on the back for being so virtuous. But experience forces me to admit that the reputed wickedness of people well known for their piety is not always exaggerated and only recently I have had renewed proof of it.

During one of my lectures I tried to show what marvellous courage a Christian is capable of when he sincerely lives his faith; as an example I told the story of a man who refused to betray his comrades and never yielded to terror, although the Germans, when eventually they arrested him, put him through the most appalling tortures, pulling his limbs from their sockets, soaking him for hours in icy water, tearing out his finger and toe nails, etc.

When I chose this example I was not doing it to stress the fact that this man has now become a prominent political figure. I was naive enough to imagine that even the people who did not share his political views would nevertheless share my admiration for the Christian virtue of courage which he had shown to such a marked degree. Alas I was not very well acquainted with the ways of bigotry.

I have just been told that a certain L. is furious with me. He is a man of spectacular piety who is also known for his extreme right-wing views. I personally have no quarrel with his views because I don't believe that the Catholic faith imposes obligations on the faithful with regard to their political opinions. Whatever political belief one holds one should uphold it in a Christian manner. But this does not seem to be the view of my co-religionists who in spite of repeated papal decrees ever since the days of Leo XIII refuse to distinguish between their religious faith and their political opinions and still insist that Christian socialists in particular are heretics.

L. did not deny that what I had said about the other man was true but he was scandalised that I praised a man who, so he maintains, is divorced and remarried; he even accused me of betraying Christian moral standards!

Even if it were true that the man in question had since become a 'public sinner' it would in no way diminish the fact that he used to lead a genuinely Christian life; but where L. reveals the utter ignominy of his bigotry is that the other man, whom I have known for the last twenty-five years, definitely is still married to the woman he married some twenty years ago. L. realising that in eyes of good Catholics nothing harms a man in public life more than the fact that he is divorced and remarried, attacks the man's private life because he does not approve of his political views. Too bad if the accusations are false!

This experience reminds me of certain unpleasant practices of the communist party. Overnight a man who, for years has been the idol of the party can become the butt of the worst insults and calumnies, simply because he no longer finds favour with his chiefs. While he was formerly praised for his exemplary family life, his devotion to the cause and his intelligence, he is suddenly accused of having no morals, of being mean, selfish and stupid. Bigots of the type of L. are no better. Without any evidence they deny the religious sincerity of those who do not share their political views, and equally without evidence they 'canonise' those who do.

1952 — 3

1952

5th February

Two days ago I lunched with a high ranking civil servant who is a Freemason. He was quite frank about his reasons for adhering to the Lodge, about the satisfaction it gives him and also about the disappointments it holds for him. In particular he complained about his 'brothers' who perpetually try to use him ever since they have found out that he holds an important position. Nor did he deny that the definition of Freemasonry which I quoted—a society of mutual badgering—was correct.

Talking to me privately he said, 'Please don't think that I feel hostile towards religion. On the contrary. Whenever I am fed up and things in my life don't go the way I want I would be so happy if I could find comfort in religion. You people who believe don't know how lucky you are—you need not worry over any awkward problem because your religion has an answer for everything.'

I was too much of a coward to disillusion him. Besides I doubt if he would have understood me if I had told him that faith in Jesus Christ does not always supply the ready made answer to all human anxieties and that the Christian does not always rest serene in the possession of truth and religion is not infallibly the consolation of the weak or the 'opium of the people'.

He certainly is not alone in sincerely believing, with a certain nostalgia, that religion is synonymous with spiritual consolation. So many tormented people have said to me: 'How lucky religious people are. If they want to know the truth and hear what they ought to do all they need do is listen to what the priest tells them.' The trouble is that evidently many Christians also think of religion as a sort of spiritual bath chair. The insults Nietzsche flung at Christianity are quite often justified if they are applied to the manner in which religion is adapted by many to suit their individual lives. (Not, of course, that that was what Nietzsche meant—his attack was against Christianity in its essence.) A few years ago a young teacher friend of mine who was an atheist but not a fanatic and was, if anything, attracted by the Christian ideal, happened to hear a well-meaning priest preach about the Miraculous Medal. What kind of idea is one to form about a religion whose priest tells you that to carry a medal—even if it is miraculous—suffices to guarantee salvation? The preacher, who probably wanted to make an impression on his audience, continued by telling the story of a man who was very surprised when, at the point of death, he saw the gates of heaven flung wide open ready to admit him, although he had lived an impious and sinful life. But here was our Lady to tell him that he was saved because, in memory of his mother, he had never omitted to recite a Hail Mary before going to sleep. Isn't that a sure way of turning people against this beautiful prayer?

Then take E. who had been for many years a militant activist of the extreme left wing and was, like so many others, disillusioned by the criminal contempt for human dignity apparent in her party's everyday actions. She broke with it and resolutely went in search of an ideal as powerful and effective as communism, but more genuinely human. I gave her the New Testament to read and immediately the figure of Christ as seen in the gospel and in St Paul's epistles appealed to her as being the perfect Leader, supremely capable of transforming the world. E. decided that she would become a Catholic and, as an initial preparation for this step she went to spend two weeks in a convent. However, a preacher chose to enlarge on Margaret Mary's visions of the Sacred Heart. He spoke of an unhappy and tearful Jesus, suffering even now (in heaven!) from men's sins, imploring the saint to have pity on him and to console him. This obviously was not the conquering hero E. was searching for and, very sadly, she left the convent. It took me a

148

very long time to explain to her how one must take those pious metaphors chiefly composed for the benefit of a certain type of suffering soul.

The true image of Christianity is continually being disfigured by a type of devout phraseology which emphasises too much the need for pity, consolation and humility and does not say enough about power, courage and the steadfast strength which should be the driving force in a Christian life. After all, although women—and what splendid women—followed Jesus, his daily companions were men whose record in no way suggests that they were effeminate fops. They were rough ordinary people who gave up everything to follow Jesus because they realised that he was able to offer their souls solid and substantial food, not an insipid diet fit only for weaklings.

The rubbish that has been spoken and written about Christian humility! It has happened in the past and it still happens time and again that ambition, Christian pride and the will to achieve something are criticised because they offend against 'humility'. But in fact it is fairly easy to see the latent pharisaism in those who profess to be humble. I know quite well that often this pharisaism remains unconscious and that the 'humble' people sincerely believe in their own humility. But only very little psychological insight is required to discover that hiding behind the mask of humility is the cowardice of the selfish or the weakness of the sick and—in most cases—the pride of those who dare not face the risks attached to every kind of action, every determination to succeed. The saints, the truly humble of heart, are neither lazy nor timorous, nor do they, under the pretext of humility, shrink from adventures and enterprises which seem sheer folly in the eyes of the world. Humility for them consists in not behaving as if they owned the gifts and talents God has entrusted to them, in not reaping for themselves the credit for their work. *Non nobis, Domine* . . .

19th March

F. a technical engineer and manager of large concern is very disturbed by a Lenten sermon he has heard which was devoted to the Christian's task of practising self-detachment. Does that mean, he asked me, that we must become totally indifferent to everything human, to every value of this world? Is it possible to seek and find in things like one's profession anything except an occasion for penance? Does toil and labour—'in the sweat of thy brow thou shalt eat bread'— forbid us to enjoy our work? And does not self-abandonment in the last resort lead us to regard as an imperfection the love and care we have for our wife and children?

If these considerations were only the result of intellectual hair splitting I wouldn't take the slightest notice of F.'s questions but I know him to be a man who takes his religion seriously and has generously responded to the call of his Master. Moreover he is by no means the only one to pose these and similar questions. There is no doubt that a large number of young Christians, trained by the Catholic Action movement, are no longer prepared to tolerate the traditional separation made by Christians between the lip service paid to the evangelical maxims and the obligation to live them in their daily lives. We no longer live in the Christian era when one often was a Catholic merely because one conformed to the Catholic society. Nowadays rather than conform to social exigencies many would prefer not to be Christians at all, and if, in spite of it, they still remain within the fold it is because they obey an imperative call from above. Consequently they either stand by the gospel and its spirit or else they refuse to claim to be Christian. It is unfortunate that so many priests are still unaware that the most sincere of the present day faithful must be able to see word and action going hand in hand and that they don't take the trouble to study the full implications of the doctrine they preach but still fancy that the gospel is designed merely to awaken fine sentiments in the people's souls. Such sentiments, however, will not lead to action.

I tried to alleviate F.'s anxiety by reading to him the wonderful passage from Teilhard de Chardin's work:

'A Christian is at the same time the most detached and the most attached of human beings. More convinced than any "wordly" man that earthly success has a deep hidden relevance and value, he none the less is confident that success is of no importance whatsoever when it is looked upon as an individual (or universal) gain independent of God. It is God and only God whom he seeks in the image of creatures. For him the interest really lies *in* the things in so far as God is really present in them . . . A religion, however miraculous, is a dead religion if it falls below the standard of human ideals. Therefore it is supremely important that every Christian should understand and give living expression to his active submission to the will of God.'

It is by loyally fulfilling his duty of growing in stature and by spreading the faith that the Christian finds the finest opportunities to practise self-abandonment, self-denial and asceticism. He need only ponder on the servant who had buried in the ground the talent with which he had been entrusted and on our Lord's rejection of him to realise that nobody has the right to starve himself and that every self-inflicted mutilation is a sin.

Furthermore as P. de Chardin expressed it so beautifully, only those who have something can renounce it and although he was primarily thinking of the riches of the intellect and of the heart, the same principle could also be applied to material riches. It seems that, judging from the example of the saints, the ordinary Christian is in danger of yielding to delusions if he attempts to set out to practise mysticism and self-abandonment before having completely and utterly given himself to God.

Easter

I have just met an old friend and comrade in arms, a famous author who for years took an active part in the battle between the oppressed of the world and those who deny them their dignity and freedom. Even when he had given up all hope of victory he still continued the struggle possibly because he saw that it was the only way he could save himself personally from playing into the hands of the oppressors. When World War II ended he had to admit defeat and then he gave up the struggle.

But this revolutionary author vainly searched for a new ideal worthy of a total personal abandonment and 'free from guile'. When he heard of my conversion to Catholicism he was so shocked that he refused to shake hands with me, but today, although he knows no more about it now than he did then, he is evidently impressed by it. As a matter of fact he admitted that he sees no salvation and no hope for mankind except in Christianity. 'But', he added sadly, 'I don't believe in it'.

This actually is the tragic problem of so many present-day intellectuals. They no longer adopt the scornful and condescending attitude of the free thinkers of a few years ago. They don't now even believe that the faith represents a refuge for weaklings who lack the courage to face the absolute nonsense of all existence. They gladly acknowledge the beauty of the Christian ideal and are eager to admire it. But, like my friend, they say they are totally unable to believe.

Could it be true that the grace of faith was being refused to someone who was searching for it? Since I cannot admit that there is a sort of predestination in matters of faith I enquired closely into my friend's difficulties in accepting the Christian message.

He is prepared to agree that Christianity inspired in the past many great and beautiful works and that for centuries it has been the driving force behind many people's life and death. But he is also firmly convinced that Christianity is inseparably bound up with one particular civilisation and regime. And since he believes this civilisation is outmoded and done with he refuses to admit that Christianity can have any except an aesthetic appeal to modern man.

I wish our conversation could have been overheard by the type of Christian in whose good faith I have no reason to doubt, but who refuses to recognise the need to detach the gospel from compromising links with any given civilisation, mentality, policy, or philosophy. No argument, no eloquence, can prove that the message of Christ is addressed to every human being, in all ages and civilisations, of every creed or philosophy. Only the Christian and his behaviour can do that. That is why I so much admire some of the Catholics of Poland and other communist-dominated countries who have tried without compromising their faith to take their full share in the new regime being created in their countries. Not that I share the naive view of some 'progressive' men who see communism as the first rung of the ladder to the Kingdom of God. No kingdom of this world is entirely of God, but it seems to me that is precisely the reason why the Church, who accepted the feudal and capitalist systems should not adopt a purely negative attitude where the communist regime is concerned. One would have to be totally ignorant of history to imagine that feudalism or capitalism were more naturally Christian than communism. Even after several centuries of co-operating with them the Church has not completely succeeded in baptising them—but that doesn't mean that her efforts have been unnecessary or wrong. Are we not making the same mistake as the communists if we believe any regime to be permanent or perfect?

It is unfortunate that influential circles in the Church have not fully appreciated the sacrificial spirit of the best of our Christian brothers of the East. Yet the Cardinal Archbishops of Warsaw and Prague were prepared to consider communism as a form of social organisation with good and bad sides. Possibly its faults are more grievous and numerous than those of other societies but could that not be an additional reason for implanting it with the seed of the gospel? The policy in Rome, influenced by the emigrated prelates who like all emigrants of all times dream of a return to the old order of things, has been to wait for the early collapse of the communist rule. This, as the people on the spot know only too well, is a mere fantasy.

I know that the strained relations between the Church and the communist states are not entirely due to the Church since the communists from the start were hostile towards the good intentions of Mgr Beran and Cardinal Wyszinsky. Nor am I trying to excuse the persecutors. But it is our duty to try to understand them. It is well known that communists are not interested in religion as such. Whether the faithful believe in God as three Persons or four or one, whether or not we believe in the Real Presence of the Holy Eucharist are, as far as the communists are concerned, a lot of idle questions. Religion is to them so alien a concept that it would not occur to them, for instance, to set up tribunals like those of ancient Rome where Christians were commanded to renounce their faith. They simply consider religion to be a phenomenon produced by a specific civilisation and the accepted economic conditions it brings in its wake. In order to overcome these prejudices and to win Christians the right of citizenship within the communist society it would have been necessary to prove beyond doubt that our faith has nothing in common with any given civilisation. But that, unfortunately, the Vatican failed to see.

However noble and specifically religious minded the motives were which prompted the Roman authorities to forbid the acceptance of a *modus vivendi* between the communist government and the Polish, Czech and Hungarian episcopates, in the eyes of millions of people in these countries—many of them Christians—it demonstrated that the Church is closely linked with the capitalist system.

17th August

Together with a few friends I went to spend the feast of the Assumption in El-Kebbab at the hermitage of Fr Peyriguère.

For the last twenty-five years the Father has lived here among the powerful Berber tribe of Ait-Ichqer. The Berbers long ago ceased to think of him as a foreigner. Watching how respectfully they greet him, how they welcome him to their tents makes one realise that here is truly the *marabout*, the saint of the Berber mountains.

I don't know which I admire more—the great austerity of his life or his immense humanity. He sleeps on a thin mat on the hard floor of his room and his food and clothing differ in no way from those of the people whose life he shares for the love of Christ. Apart from the hours he sets aside for reading and study nothing in his life seems, humanly speaking, in the least attractive. But there is nothing in Father Peyriguère's attitude remotely suggestive of bigotry. He has not even completely renounced his claim to be a 'man of the world'. After leading us to his garden where we were to pitch our tents he turned with a charming smile and offered the 'corner where the lilac grows' to the ladies. With true Berber—and French—hospitality he gave a dinner in our honour in no way resembling his usual fare. And when it was his turn to be our guest he accepted with alacrity the feast Madame B., our marvellous cook, had prepared. During meals he was gay and witty.

A young girl of our company who had not practised her religion for years was so charmed by his sanctity and humanity that she asked him to hear her confession so that she could take up her faith again and stay here to care for the sick and the poor. But the Father has too much experience in the direction of souls to trust the fervour of new converts. Therefore he preferred to treat her request as a joke and gently teased her about it.

After a few days in Father Peyriguère's company one can hardly believe that the high administrative officials of the Protectorate regard him as a traitor to his country. One governor in particular, himself a practising Catholic, recently did all he could to obtain permission to expel the Father. Yet the love and devotion Fr Peyriguère has for France are at least as great as those of a fanatical patriot. But his main purpose in life is to teach the Berbers to love Christ and to bring him to them. He also hopes that his presence amongst them will increase their love for France and if at frequent intervals he must oppose his country's official representatives it is because, more from stupidity than wickedness, they discredit and abuse him. The Berbers are a proud people—even in rags they carry themselves with dignity—and to treat them with arrogance and contempt as so many officials do is a serious disservice to the France the civil servants are supposed to represent.

Typical is a story of a young Moslem friend, a contributor to my paper who worked as interpreter in an office for native affairs. The bishop arrived to administer Confirmation and Mohammed asked if he might pay him his respects, a reasonable request since he had met the bishop several times in my office. But the head of the department, a good Catholic, replied: 'You—a Moslem? Our bishop is none of your business!'

But part of Father Peyriguère's clash with officialdom comes from his great admiration of the Berber civilisation. The Ait-Ichqer are a semi-nomadic tribe and while the Protectorate makes every effort to induce them to settle down the Father opposes such endeavours because, as he explained to us, he realises how intimately the Berber customs and habits, their language and rich poetry are linked with their semi-nomadic life. He fears that an urban life would unsettle them like people who are cut off from their living traditions. The administration on the other hand maintains that, thanks to the progress in hygiene and preventive medicine (largely due incidentally to Father Peyriguère's own efforts), the increase in population is so great that the traditional pastoral economy can no longer support it. The ground, if methodically tilled, would give ample return but that would mean the end of their nomadic life. Each of the two parties is right, of course, from his own particular point of view.

As far as missionary 'statistics' go Father Peyriguère has had no 'success' whatsoever. In the course of twenty-five years he has not converted one single Berber to Christianity, nor even tried to do so. He explained to us that under present conditions the Christian missionary must not attempt to convert the Moroccan Moslems because such a convert would necessarily be exposed to criticism from his people and would eventually be excluded from the Moslem community. As yet the Berbers have not arrived at the stage where each of them is aware of his individual conscience and thus he would be unable to fulfil his human destiny outside the community. Since they regard Christianity as the religion of the conquering alien the convert would appear as a traitor to his people and the missionary would be regarded as the agent of the oppressor.

The Father is not troubled by his lack of conversions but is very disturbed by the laxity his Berbers show with regard to the Moslem faith. He can see no benefit for either Christians or Moslems in the steady progress of materialism which, in practice if not in theory, is invading tribal life and he continually exhorts them to be good Moslems.

As for converting them to Christianity that can only come about in the course of time. For the moment the missionaries can only imitate St John the Baptist and prepare the way.

20th October

I invited Lanza del Vasto to give a series of lectures in Morocco. The halls were filled to capacity because even here Hinduism is very fashionable although I must admit that the audience consisted mainly of Frenchmen, the Moslems being few and far between.

It is a good thing for Christians to be reminded that the divine Spirit works wonders of sanctity and love in the whole world, even outside the boundaries of the visible Church. Furthermore Lanza deliberately wears the cross of Christ on his breast to demonstrate that it was as a Christian that he went to India for 'restoration' and—in his quality as a Christian —became a disciple of Ghandi.

But I was sad to find that Vasto is no longer content to be the great poet he is but affects to be a *gourou*, a teacher. It seems to me that he radiated so much more greatness and genuineness in the days when he was simply an artist and sang his own poetry to the accompaniment of his guitar. Now he is trying to make disciples and to transmit a message and he no longer reflects the peace one expects a religious teacher to have. He is too perturbed and gives an impression of insincerity. At least that was the verdict of most of the discerning people who met him during his stay in Morocco. Certainly he made a few 'disciples' but nearly all of the kind of poor wrecked soul who is always following a new false prophet of the abstruse.

One evening at the house of one of my friends my hostess suddenly asked me whether I could make Lanza abandon his role of prophet and simply be himself, the poet. For the next half hour or so, with superb skill, he recited a number of his poems for us, and, for the first time since his arrival in Morocco he captured the hearts of all present. I am convinced that it was on this occasion that he rendered the best service to the cause so dear to him. So I was amazed when next morning he rebuked me for having induced him to act a part which no longer corresponded to his present personality. It is a great pity.

18th December

Earlier this month Morocco was the scene of events which may have great significance for the future of the country. It is difficult to find out exactly what happened in Casablanca the morning of December 7th when a general strike was called because of the assassination, by individuals in the pay of the colonists, of Fehrat Hached, the Tunisian trade union leader. It was intended merely to stage a peaceful demonstration and we shall probably never know how this developed into a riot. For the past few months the nationalist parties have been publishing violent anti-French propaganda and it was inevitable that sooner or later the masses would air their hostile feelings. The official version of the incident insists that the police only intervened after some Europeans had been killed. Many people however—not only the Moroccan nationalists—are convinced that the riot was instigated by one high official in particular, a rabid reactionary, who wanted an excuse to bring the national movement to heel and to nip in the bud the growing trade unions. The Machiavellis of colonialism are said to have incited the police to provoke the masses.

This version is most probably the true one in view of the fact that the colonial press launched a campaign of false news telling of numerous French women raped by Moroccans, ten Europeans killed by natives and large quantities of arms seized and the difficulty of preventing rioting masses from 'descending' upon the European quarter of the town. All these things were proved false and although it is true that several Europeans were killed it is not at all certain that they were killed by the rioters. And dozens—I have been told hundreds—of Moroccans were killed by the police.

However the worst thing is the wave of racial hatred that has become apparent through these events in Casablanca. When the police arrested the militant trade-unionists a number of French women went for the defenceless men; most of these women were working class which shows how colonialism has stifled the feeling of solidarity among the exploited masses and substituted a racial superiority complex among the Europeans.

The majority of Catholics have toed the party line. I heard one good Franciscan Father telling a group of men from his parish how to restore peace and harmony in Morocco. All that was needed was to shoot all natives who had passed their examinations and acquired some knowledge, to suppress the schools and only then to preach the duty of charity and good will to the colonists and other leaders. One solitary voice was heard to remonstrate.

20th February

I had lunch in Paris with Pastor N. and several leading Protestant personalities. All these Christians are firmly convinced that the Vatican is deliberately trying to prevent understanding between the various denominations and sabotage the ecumenical movement. They have read *Humani Generis*, particularly the passages which pass censure on 'irenism'. They also know that a remarkable work by a Dominican—an expert on the reform movement—has been withdrawn from circulation because it does not sufficiently attack the 'heretics'; but in particular they take the recent definition of the dogma of the Assumption as a direct thrust at the Protestants, aimed at nipping in the bud all attempts to come to terms with the Catholics. According to them the prevailing mentality in 'Rome' is specifically totalitarian. They maintain that whilst the Vatican is much in favour of a reunion of all Christians this is conceived in terms of an unconditional surrender to the Church of Rome by Protestants, Anglicans and Orthodox alike. In order that the submission should be especially humiliating— so they argue—the Vatican invents dogmas and devotions which run counter to the beliefs of non-Catholics.

Naturally I contradicted them pointing out that the definition of the dogma of the Assumption was in no way a hostile act against Protestants but that when the dogma was proclaimed the Vatican simply was not considering Protestants at all. That, in fact, is one of the Church's tragedies. Although the believing and practising Catholics form a small portion of the world's population the Roman administration behaves as if the whole world were subject to it, simply because it persists in remaining in that spiritual ghetto so characteristic of the leading circles of the Church. They play at believing in Christian civilisation although in fact Christian civilisation has disappeared and may never appear again.

I feel sure that many things would change if the Church leaders were really conscious of our being a minority in the world. They would insist less on certain types of ceremonies and ecclesiastical style which in the eyes of the present generation do little credit to the religion and are a major obstacle to conversions. I am not so naive as to believe the tastes and spontaneous reactions of men of the twentieth century are more important than those of previous generations and it would be absurd to expect the Church of God to conform to the changing tastes of the times. But I would like to see the Church not brushing aside completely these tastes and reactions because after all she has to bring the message of salvation to men and women of this generation as much as to any other and not to an abstract humanity.

The same applies to the definition of the dogma of the Assumption. Several famous theologians and saintly bishops advised against the definition, not because they doubted the truth of the dogma but simply because the definition seemed, for the moment, inopportune. They had reason to believe it might prejudice non-Catholics and also have a restrictive influence in matters of faith. The Christian tradition has never professed that the only valid articles of our faith are dogmas which have been solemnly defined. Generally in the past the Councils advised such definitions as a means of settling debates amongst Catholic theologians. But since for many centuries no theologian within the Church has contested the validity of the Assumption defining it as a dogma was bound to make non-Catholics think the Church considers only defined dogmas as articles of faith. Such an implication could have disastrous consequences since some fundamental religious truths have never been defined.

It seems to me that the spiritual efficacy of the Church in the present world could be greatly enhanced if more emphasis were placed on the essentials of the Christian message. At the moment alas the exact opposite seems to be the case. Catholics, possibly too timorous to face the realities of the world as it is are perpetually inventing new devotions and enthusing over miracles and apparitions. No wonder that men engaged in the struggle for existence see Christianity not as a renewing force but as an anachronistic survival of days gone by. And as I have been able to observe on so many occasions, prominent Churchmen do not even suspect that this playing at Christendom isolates them from the rest of the world.

11th April

The attitude taken by a large number of Catholics over the riots last December and the repercussions they had for the natives does great credit to the Christian cause. Those Frenchmen in Morocco who have had the courage to dissociate themselves publicly from the wave of racial hatred sweeping the country are mostly Catholics. One of my friends wanted to organise a public collection amongst Frenchmen in aid of the victims of the punitive measures and their families but he had to abandon the plan because the authorities would have regarded it not as an act of charity but as deliberate provocation and would have refused permission. Nevertheless the Christians have found ways of quietly doing their duty in accordance with the fundamental demands of the gospel.

The courageous way in which Mauriac spoke up for the Moroccans in *Figaro* has raised a terrible storm among colonialists who have branded him as an enemy of France and spread the rumour that he received fabulous sums from the Sultan and the Moroccan nationalist party. The reporters of *Figaro* and the leaders of intellectual Catholic circles in France who also objected to the treatment of the Moroccans are similarly accused of taking bribes, particularly if their version of events differed from the official one. Apparently perfectly honest people living under a scheme of colonial exploitation cannot conceive that men can act disinterestedly or from other motives than gain.

But the reputation of the Church has been greatly enhanced

by the number of people who have openly proclaimed truth and justice more important than national solidarity. The bishop himself, although remaining rigorously unpolitical, wrote a remarkable pastoral letter reminding Catholics in no uncertain terms of their duty in this land of Islam. The Nationalist parties had the pastoral translated into Arabic and widely distributed in all the assemblies. Henceforth perhaps Moroccan Moslems will see in the Christian religion more than a mere ideological superstructure of colonialism.

The aggravating thing is that Mauriac and other Christians in Paris who denounce the crimes of colonialism are completely ignorant of what life in Morocco is like. They defend the right principles but base their defence on incorrect facts and consequently make it very awkward for those who are working on the spot and are engaged in proclaiming the principles and putting them into practice. The colonial spokesmen win arguments merely by pointing to the false statement made by Mauriac and the others. It is a very short step from this to alleging that the principle is wrong also and as it is identical with our principle we are dismissed as impractical dreamers.

13th April

The consequences of the riots affect not only Moroccans. The Nationalist leaders have been imprisoned or exiled in the desert miles away from the towns and many liberal Frenchmen have been listed and punished as traitors because they made the effort to establish friendly relations with the Moslems instead of trying to subdue them. One retired officer, disabled in World War I and greatly respected by the natives among whom he has lived for years has even been expelled from Morocco. The protest I made about it in *Maroc Monde* brought me a deluge of letters. Because the officer is not a Catholic I am accused of making common cause with an 'enemy of Holy Church'; several correspondents demanding publication of their letters under threat of withdrawing their subscriptions pretend to reveal facts about his private life.

Naturally I refused to publish them. It is not for his morals he has been expelled from Morocco but for his political conduct. If readers don't share his political views they ought at least to have the courage to say so instead of taking the much easier course of attacking his private life since every word can serve to insinuate things and it is practically impossible to defend oneself. It is a type of infamy which, alas, is very popular with some Christians.

6th May

It is unfortunate for the Moroccan cause that many of the Catholic 'personalities' who are interested in the course of events are not of the same calibre as Mauriac and those inspired solely by love of justice. Following an unofficial invitation from the resident governor a delegation of 'Catholic Members of Parliament' has arrived here on a tour of investigation. I wonder how much they hope to discover about the real position in a country about which up to now they knew nothing at all. Shepherded by an old Colonel, an honest but extremely narrow-minded man, they attend two banquets per day. The rest of the day is spent driving about in official cars across the country and being shown the points of interest and 'achievements'—the benefits of which are reserved for tourists.

However it is a favourable sign that the organisers of the 'delegation' were only able to find a single genuinely Catholic M.P. prepared to join. The others are from the ranks of the radicals and have been labelled 'Catholic' for this particular purpose. But also taking part in the tour is the editor of a weekly, unofficially Catholic, paper.

The journalist seems to be the only one who is trying to make contacts outside the official ones. I arranged a meeting between him and a group of active Christians from the working and middle classes, who gave him a fair and honest account of the facts of the situation. Before leaving my office he assured us that he had understood all we had told him and indeed gave us a very intelligent summary of all he had learnt.

Alas, I have just read his 'report' published in his own paper. His honesty does not seem to match his intelligence. He 'reports' exactly the opposite of what we gathered he 'understood', even enlarging on the official version whose falseness he admitted to me and my friends. But there it is. Possibly after he had left us he was persuaded that it is not always 'expedient' to tell the truth and that there are reasons of state which justify lying, even if one is a Catholic.

28th August

Morocco has just witnessed a tragi-comedy. The men behind the administration and the native feudal leaders have carried out a coup resulting in the deposition of the Sultan and the setting up in office of an old man who will be too weary to want to embarrass the intriguers, schemers, profiteers.

The new Sultan's entry into Rabat was indeed a tragic sight. There were very few Moslems about but the French population was there in force giving him an enthusiastic welcome. By the grace of M. Juin and the prefect of police the ruler of Morocco has become the 'great friend of France', the guardian of French interests in Morocco.

What depresses me is the behaviour of so many priests in this upheaval. The bishop, as always, is dignified and courageous in his refusal to participate at the official ceremonies and the high officials are very displeased with him. Most priests, on the other hand, seized the opportunity to celebrate an event which, they hope, will appreciably benefit both the Church and the Protectorate for in their confused minds they take these interests to be one and the same.

It is not easy to swim against the stream. Almost every Frenchman in Morocco is convinced that the good old times are back and that at least for the next twenty years nothing will stand in their way, or in other words, will prevent them accumulating great wealth at the expense of the natives. I have tried to explain to my compatriots in carefully worded articles that such a hope is a fantasy and that the new Sultan and his French helpers are not genuine leaders. This has produced an uproar and letters announcing the cancellation of subscriptions flood the office; the Dean of Morocco, who knows full well that the paper has the whole-hearted support of the bishop, has attacked us from the pulpit and delivered a homily in praise of the new Sultan.

Yet the moment the sexual moral code is in question the priests and all good tradition-minded Catholics are very meticulous. They campaign against moral laxity in young people, against divorce, adultery, abortion and contraception. Yet they must know that the brothels of Morocco are one of the new Sultan's principal sources of income, that crimes are committed in his harem and that he is a tyrant in his dealings with the tribes under his command. But because his political views—not very admirable ones at that—favour colonialism and materialism these people turn a blind eye to his crimes and his immorality and hail him as a 'saintly old man, the friend of France'. If it were only the colonists and the business men among the Catholics who act thus it would be forgivable but when priests join in this cult it becomes a matter for concern. Fortunately there are still men like the bishop and Father Peyriguère and a few other priests and there are valiant Christian lay people in increasing numbers who see and protest at what is going on: one can only hope that the people of Morocco will not blame the Church of Christ for the blunders made by her wealthy sons.

9th November

My friends with whom I discuss things and many people who write to me are perturbed at the perceptible widening of the gulf between the Church and the common run of mankind. I need only leave the sacristy and cross the border of the Catholic ghetto to notice how small the space is which people assign to God in their daily lives and worldly preoccupations. In fact it is so small that high-minded men and women seem to have every reason to consider him to be an unessential luxury. Certain Christians even wonder whether it would not be more 'honest' to renounce all religious proselytising temporarily and use their entire strength to help with the construction of the new world and be ready to evangelise it when it is finally brought into being.

The Dominican founder of *Jeunesse d'Eglise* recently wrote a pamphlet on this question. It was censored by the hierarchy but the problems it discussed are still there. From what I see and hear it even seems that they are uppermost in many people's minds.

The gist of his argument is approximately: the Capitalist world has become so hideous that only very exceptional people are capable of living a genuine Christian life in it. Many people and particularly the workers believe that we must build a new world in its place. Their energies are all directed to that one aim and talking to them about God, redemption and eternal salvation appears to them as a dangerous diversion; only Marxism apparently indicates the road to be taken and furnishes modern man with the necessary ideological weapons for the realisation of his urgent task of creating a human society on communist lines. Since experience shows that the Christian influence has a paralysing effect on the workers' fighting spirit it is in the interest of mankind and the Church that the spreading of this influence should be curtailed; only when the new communist society is established will it be possible to preach the gospel's purest spirit and that will be the moment when the Church can undertake its great task of preaching to mankind the eternal salvation in Christ; in the meantime she must be content to prepare the way for a future spreading of the gospel; only by adding his full strength to the struggle and triumph of the social revolution is the present-day Christian able to acquit himself of his precursory mission.

Now of course the bishops and the Vatican could not condone such a suggestion. Moreover the good Father and his friends are hopelessly ill-informed if they allot to Marxist communism the readiness or the power to prepare the way for a future spreading of the Christian message. The situation, for Christians as well as for others, is tragic because although communism is almost the only truly revolutionary force in existence today, it cannot liberate mankind from present-day slavery for the simple reason that, being just as materialistic and anti-humane as capitalism, it is anti-capitalist only in appearance; in fact it is the capitalist system run riot.

Stating these facts unfortunately does not provide a positive solution to the distress expressed by the author of the pamphlet and shared by so many Christians. I can hardly argue against his contention that the Church is no longer *up to date* and that she speaks a language and is engaged in activities which are incomprehensible to the broad masses of this generation. How petty our study circles, our support of 'social works' must seem to people who are concerned with world problems. How little the 'stating of principles' and the hierarchy's pious exhortations correspond to the deep uneasiness felt by so many modern men and women.

Like many others I used to believe that the Church was about to throw off the dust of centuries and be rejuvenated and able to provide the modern world with the living spirit it so sorely needs. The tendency during Pius XI's pontificate, the *Mission de France*, the worker priest movement, new schemes encouraged by the hierarchy, the intellectual ferment furthered by theologians, philosophers and Catholic scholars of France, all seemed so hopeful. Alas we know what has happened since then.

Does this mean that we must join forces with those who are so discouraged that they wish the Church to be involved in a communist revolution which they know can only be detrimental to mankind in general? It is true they don't expect the Church to benefit from communism but they argue that it would free her from her cumbersome administrative apparatus and detach her from a society which holds her captive and which she has never been able to Christianise. They feel that after a lengthy period during which the Communist regime would undoubtedly inflict great suffering and persecution the system would invariably collapse and then the Church would be able to rise with new vigour and all the wiser for the distressing experiences of the past.

I cannot accept this desperate and heart-breaking vision of the Church's immediate future even if, to a certain extent, it is inspired by St Augustine's *City of God*. I find the politics of impending doom repulsive and instead I make an act of faith in Christ's promise to keep his Church invincible. But I have to admit that humanly speaking I cannot imagine how she can recover the ground she has lost and close the appalling gulf separating her from the world.

1954 — 6

6th January

I am in Tlemcen having just given the first of a series of lectures I am to give throughout Algeria. My theme is *Christians face Islam* which is very much to the point in North Africa and I was not surprised to see many Moslems, particularly young people, in the audience.

Without trying to blur the characteristic attributes of each of the two monotheistic religions I pointed out how much they had in common. There is the adherence to the same biblical revelation, the 'faith of Abraham' the belief in one God etc. I know that in the past Christians and Moslems have often faced each other as enemies and that there have been crusades and holy wars against Moslem rule but, looking back, it seems a reasonable conjecture that more often than not religion served as a pretext for very materialist causes and ambitions. When Mohammed, the founder of Islam first began to teach he seems to have been looked upon as yet another leader of a new Christian sect, all the more so as he lived and taught in regions where sects were many and varied. In any case the first Moslems sought and found shelter with the Christian king of Ethiopia when their Arab compatriots persecuted them. Many passages of the Koran glorify Jesus and his holy Mother and stress the need for a good understanding between Moslems and Christians. It was only when the Arab nations united under the banner of Islam and attacked Byzanz (which claimed to be the defender of Christendom) that the relations between the two religious communities deteriorated. In the course of the next centuries hatred prevented the parties from acquiring a thorough knowledge of each other's claims and gradually prejudice and ignorance increased to such an extent that they formed an insurmountable wall between Christians and Moslems. But since modern man has a deeper sense of universality and since materialistic atheism is as much a danger to Christianity as to every other religion, the moment has come, particularly here in North Africa, to destroy the last traces of hatred and rivalries of the past. It is not a question of somehow amalgamating Islam and the Christian faith but simply of replacing the attitude of the crusades and holy wars by a spirit of mutual understanding. The better the understanding the more loyal the people will be to their respective faith . . .

It seems that some Christians are not at all pleased with my talk. They accuse me of being 'irenistic', of showing too much good will to the Moslems and sapping the 'moral foundations' of colonialism. But it seems typical of the grumblers that not one of them raised his voice during the lecture to criticise my ideas whereas a large number of Christians as well as Moslems voiced their full approval. Are the colonists and the dogmatists ashamed to speak up?

A Moslem student asked 'Did I understand you to say that the era of crusades and holy wars is definitely finished and done with?' When I confirmed this he continued: 'I agree with you but did not a certain prominent Catholic politician recently proclaim that in Morocco the Cross had vanquished the Crescent?'

He is quite right. Not so long ago the Minister for Foreign Affairs, questioned in the National Assembly about the armed intervention in Rabat, replied with that phrase. As if Juin and the Prefect, still less the new Sultan, were concerned with the triumph of the Cross of Christ. The Minister's *bon mot* deeply offended the Moslems of North Africa and maybe of the whole world. I wish politicians would learn to guard their tongues.

16th January

I have been in Algeria two weeks now and am very conscious of latent unrest. Many Frenchmen seem to be unaware of it and pretend that last August's change of French politics in Morocco not only put things in order in the Protectorate but also eliminated all dangerous elements in Algeria. This feeling of security apparently encourages many French people to behave in an arrogant and conceited manner which is bound to provoke the natives' anger.

This time I am in closer touch with Algerian Moslems than I have been before and the first thing that struck me was how well informed they are about Moroccan affairs and that they realise that I belong to the group of Christians who have dissociated themselves from the crimes committed against the Moroccan people. That probably also accounts for the large number who turn up at my lectures and for the numerous invitations and visits I receive. But above all, as far as I can see, people are merely deceiving themselves if they think the Algerians are resigned to the present state of affairs in their country and have no other ambitions than to be assimilated as French citizens. It is quite evident that Algerians as well as Moroccans are gradually shaking off their 'colonisability'. When I had the chance to speak to high administrative officials I tried to make them see that an intelligent and bold policy could still avert the crisis but that, in a few months' time, they might have missed their chance. But I find that even with the most intelligent representatives of France the armed intervention in Morocco has bred a false sense of security. If only I could believe that my fears are groundless.

9th February

We have come to the end of the beautiful experiment of the worker priests. A few people hope that the French hierarchy, most of whom realise the importance of the scheme, will still be able to stem the tide but I very much doubt it. More and more the Roman *curia* lends a willing ear to the pleas of the dogmatists whose antagonism to 'progressive' Christian elements has only grown greater with success.

In the Marxist sense I too am a worker priest because for many years I have not lived from the alms of the faithful but from my work. However, mine is intellectual work and the Christian mystique applies the term work in its proper sense only to manual work, executed with sweat on the brow and under duress. But that attitude has not prevented me from the very beginning of their mission feeling deeply akin with the worker priests. No doubt it is partly because I lacked the courage as well as because I am totally incapable of doing manual work that I did not join them. It would be childish to maintain that they did not make mistakes and that all the accusations laid at their door are without foundation. Most of them had never had any dealings with the working class and knew nothing of the problems involved. Even those who originated from it had grown away from it during the time spent in the hothouse of the seminary. Pure generous Christianity having called them to share the workers' living conditions they experienced a severe shock when confronted with the reality. Small wonder if some of them failed to master the situation and rebelled.

All the same it is the first time since the deplorable gulf opened between Christianity and popular masses (according to Pius XI the greatest crime perpetrated by the capitalist era), that the Church has been given a real chance to convey the message of the gospel to the workers. Priests performing manual work is nothing new—they have been doing it to a greater or less extent ever since the days of St Paul and in many religious orders manual work is still enforced as a strictly observed rule. Living with the workers soon convinced these young priests that the modern worker is no longer the poor creature the middle classes imagine him to be. The days are gone when he gave way to despair and mulishly submitted to oppression. He is conscious of his lot but equally conscious of his power and his role in the history of mankind. The priests soon realised that however important manual work was it was even more essential that they should share the workers' living conditions, their insecurity, their hopes and struggles. That these hopes and struggles are prominent in the programme of the communist party is certainly not the fault of the worker priests, or for that matter, of the working classes as a whole.

Several worker priests, insufficiently trained for their mission and knowing next to nothing about Marxism or communism, apparently succumbed to the dangerous fascination emanating from these philosophies. They did not realise that normally the proletariat is Marxist and communist only as a result of historical developments; they were led to believe that Marxism is the inherent philosophy of the workers and that therefore they can be saved only by the Christians adopting communism. These priests were sadly deluded but I still believe that the mistakes they made are insignificant compared to the positive achievement of the experiment. Maybe their actions have not contributed to the conversion of many workers to Catholicism but for the first time in generations the working people have felt that Christ and his Church are not necessarily on the side of power and wealth. No one with an open mind can ignore the extraordinary importance this has for the evangelisation of the world in general and the poor in particular.

I have been told that the Cardinal Archbishop of Paris was staggered when he saw the large number of workers' delegations converging on his palace from all the districts where the worker priests had been engaged. Was it not the best proof of the efficacy of the mission that men and women, mostly avowed atheists and communists, went to plead with the Archbishop not to take from them the worker priests in whom they had such confidence. I am convinced that, had the Archbishop had the power, he would have given way to those of his children who, from appearances, are furthest removed from Christ.

Apparently the French bishops have obtained permission from Rome to continue the workers' mission in spite of everything that was said against it. The priests will only work a few hours per day and their movements will be closely watched by the hierarchy. The intentions of those who devised this project are undoubtedly excellent but at the same time they reveal complete misunderstanding of the workers' psychology.

The admirable success of the worker priests was due to the fact that they were not restricted, that the Holy Ghost seemed to guide them without intermediary. Rightly or wrongly the common people regard the Pope and the bishops as belonging to the well-to-do classes of the world. Are they not present at all the official ceremonies, rubbing shoulders with statesmen and leading men of industry and commerce? The opposition between the classes, however much it is to be deplored, is nevertheless still a fact. If the workers know that the missionaries act with the official approval of the Church they will immediately suspect them of being a sort of reactionary 'fifth column'. The removal of the worker priests will confirm this opinion because no worker, however fervent a Christian and active a Catholic he may be, really believes that these priests were removed for religious reasons. They are convinced that the motive is to be found in the hierarchy's political interests. We know this argument in such a form is not true but it will take years to overcome this latest prejudice against the Church.

It is disgraceful and hideously pharisaical to accuse the worker priests of mixing in politics. Since the beginning of Christianity priests have acted in the parliaments of many lands. Without going back even as far as Richelieu and Dupanloup, what about Mgr Kaas in Germany, Mgr Tisza in Slovakia, Canon Desgranges and Canon Kir in France, all of whom have held high positions in the political life of their countries in recent times? Does the fact that these eminent ecclesiastics occupy Conservative seats suffice to absolve them of the sin of mixing in politics?

10th March

There is great commotion in intellectual circles. Rome has relieved of their office all three French Dominican provincials and replaced them by men who are expected to be more docile with regard to the Church's new course of action. But what is even worse than the provincials' removal from office—after all that is an internal affair of the Dominicans—is the disgrace of several members of the same Order which many people feel is like a slap in the face. Through their writings and spirit these men have guided untold numbers of men and women towards the Church. Together with a certain number of priests, both secular and religious, they were for many a kind of symbol for the reconciliation between the Church and the modern world.

It is not altogether without significance that non-Catholics and even atheists are also concerned at the blow directed against Fathers Avril, Boisselot, Chenu, Congar and the others. The dismissal of Fr Congar particularly is resented by the Protestants who argue, rightly or wrongly, that by disgracing this apostle of unity Rome is undermining his attempts to reconcile the various Christian creeds with each other.

I have seen a copy of the letter P. Avril wrote to *Amitiés Dominicains*. Without disguising his deep sadness or minimising the harm this latest triumph of the dogmatists is likely to do to the cause of religion in France the former Father Provincial gives evidence of a wonderful spirit of religious obedience. Whilst he agrees that 'our general attitude with regard to present day apostolic problems has for some time been the subject of criticism, attacks and denunciations' he and his brethren submit to the decision of their Superior. I have an idea that the dogmatists must be rather irritated by this obedience because it deprives their ignominious campaign of all likelihood of truth.

10th October

Some friends invited me to spend a few days in a village near the border in Alsace Lorraine and I took the opportunity to have a closer look at the life of the Church in a district which still enjoys all the privileges and material advantages accorded to its inhabitants by the Concordat of 1802. I have quite a number of aquaintances amongst priests and laymen, Catholics, Protestants and atheists and I was asked to attend various ecclesiastical functions and reunions where I could listen to what the people had to say and see how they reacted to various problems.

The first thing that struck me was the relative comfort in which the clergy live. They are by no means rich because the payment allotted to priests by the State is more or less on the same level as that allotted to teachers, but in addition they benefit from the generosity of the faithful which, in this traditionally Catholic country is fairly large so that, compared with the conditions of the French clergy in the country, the Alsatian priests seem to be materially very well off indeed.

What kind of effect does this well-being have on the recruitment of priests? Evidently vocations are more numerous than in districts where a man who wants to be a priest must be prepared to be poor, sometimes even miserably poor. Some people complain that their priests are very mediocre because the consideration of the material advantages has outweighed the spiritual grandeur of the priesthood. It is also said that families often decide that one of their sons is to be a priest without giving him the opportunity to choose for himself. My personal observation didn't really enable me to judge one way or the other.

However I found that a large majority of the priests are devoid of culture or intellectual interests. They even seem unconcerned with apostolic problems and discharge their duties like good civil servants. The Christians who have lived in different parts of France speak of the poor quality of the sermons delivered here and of the sheer impossibility of receiving spiritual aid from the priests. And certainly it seems that authoritarian clericalism is even more noticeable than in the country parishes of Britanny.

There is the case of the active Christian in Alsace who, in order to introduce the Christian spirit into an organisation, joined a non-Catholic trade union. The following Sunday the parish priest devoted the whole of his sermon to the denunciation of 'these traitors to the holy faith' who 'join organisations not approved of or supervised by the Church'.

A large number of priests are engaged in political struggles and sit on general and municipal councils. They have no scruples about ordering their flock to vote for one particular party and they take an active part in election campaigns. One priest, a councillor of the Moselle district, told me how he ran his own electoral campaign by distributing rosaries and holy pictures. He was even annoyed with one of his friends because he refused to do the same and thus lost several thousand votes during the last general election. It is important to remember that these men are acting in the best of faith, that the thought has never crossed their minds that it might not be legitimate to identify religion with a certain type of political tradition. Needless to say in this district a priest would be considered as a sort of apostate if he were to show sympathy for progressive ideas.

Each of these priests considers himself to be the 'guardian' of morality even if he has only a very hazy idea of his people's spiritual life. Does this alertness for moral dangers result in a higher moral level of behaviour compared with other regions? Possibly yes, particularly in country districts and particularly with regard to sexual and marital morals. Divorce is practically unknown and the same applies to sexual relations between young men and girls. But irregularities do still occur because several priests told me that 'forced' marriages are frequently contracted. It is of course a moot point whether the apparently high moral tone is due to the priest's vigilance or social pressure.

I have too little experience of life in Christian countries to be able to assess the objective value of things which surprise me. Thus I am astonished that the resident priest of a public hospital is incapable of understanding that he has no right, under the pretext of being the moral guardian, to subject the private and public lives of doctors, nurses and patients to a sort of police supervision. But apparently he is exceptional even in this traditionally Catholic part because he is cordially disliked by everyone.

I am most interested in the educational problems of these regions. Since all the schools are denominational I asked priests, teachers and parents what they thought about it. The teachers complain of having to lead prayers and teach religion. Oddly enough the practising Catholics complain as much as the non-believers. The Catholics contend that religion, taught like any other subject, must necessarily endanger the✓ children's appreciation of its sacred character. They also maintain that many priests are reluctant to teach it themselves because they are either too lazy or too ignorant. Among the priests all but three of those whom I met were greatly in favour of the existing system. When during an official ecclesiastical dinner I had the temerity to be sceptical about the value of a religion taught by unbelieving lay teachers and to question the hypocrisy they are thus forced to adopt I was told 'If these teachers don't believe our holy faith they can go and teach elsewhere; if they choose to remain here they must accept the local custom.'

Does what I have seen and heard entitle me to draw critical conclusions regarding the specific privileges of the Church in Alsace Lorraine? I hesitate because I know so little about traditionally Catholic regions and I cannot judge whether the things I have seen here are a consequence of the Concordat or simply the result of the social structure of the district.

The German speaking Catholics seem to accept the prevailing situation readily whereas the French speaking people are less conformist and certainly very critical of religious life in this part. This may be due to frequent communication with other parts of France. But it does seem that most of the priests have not even noticed that their own refusal to keep abreast of happenings in other countries may sooner or later have disastrous consequences.

Indeed I felt that the customs and way of life and mentality

182

in Alsace Lorraine are already undergoing a transformation. A religion set in the formula of a dead past is no longer in harmony with the reality which the young people, Christian ✓ and non-Christian, must face. I admit that in principle these priests and their faithful value and cling to their exceptional position and privileges and who am I to call on them to abolish them. But they will have to be more aware of the state of the modern world if they want to avoid a disastrous religious dilemma in a future more immediate than they realise. In particular they will have to break themselves of many pleasant habits and renew their apostolic and teaching methods.

12th October

In recent years many French priests have left holy orders and returned to the world. I know that the ecclesiastical authorities do not like to broadcast this but it is so generally known by now that there is little point in hushing it up.

I am not thinking of men who have left holy orders for purely personal reasons. There have always been some and their affairs are between themselves and God. But there are the worker priests who thought that they must choose between their loyalty to the workers' world and their obedience to the new ruling of the hierarchy, and the intellectuals who, discouraged by the persecutions and calumnies to which the dogmatists expose them, are under the impression that their superiors lend a willing ear to the latter, and there are even some who have been led to believe in Marxist dialectics and thought that they could no longer belong to a Church which condemned Marxism. Some of them lost their faith (they constitute a small minority) whilst the others believe in the Church and suffer cruelly from being outside it.

Last night I met some of these men. A number of them used to be in the vanguard of the Church's action in France. They held important posts and were well accredited with their bishops, even with the Vatican. They are not married except for one man; several of them even continue to practise their religion as ordinary faithful. Rome having refused official permission for them to be reinstated as laymen they regard themselves as being *temporarily without ministry* and are prepared to take it up again as soon as the prevailing spirit has given way to a better comprehension of the spiritual needs of our time; in other words as soon as the Church realises that it must break away from a society which they consider to be historically doomed.

All these men have one thing in common: not one of them seems to have found joy or peace of mind. Some pretend to be happy and wonder how they were able for so many years to bear the burden of priestly obligations but I sense bitterness in their aggressiveness towards the Church and its leaders. Their words don't ring true and I am convinced that, at the bottom of their hearts, they regret their lost functions. It certainly seems as if not one of them took the decisive step in a fit of weakness or on the spur of the moment but that they all felt that their duty, their loyalty to themselves and their vocation called for the break.

One of them used to be a worker priest and his dedication was such that in the borough where he lived his name was as famous as that of the priest hero in Cesbron's novel. I had the privilege of seeing him at work and admired the respect and confidence extended to him by a proletariat with strong Marxist leanings. When Rome and his bishop ordered him to leave the factory and the *quartier* he did not see how he could do it and when he was urged to comply he publicly broke with the Church. Convinced that it was his personality which attracted his comrades he naturally decided to serve them as assiduously as before and he thought that by marrying he would be even nearer to them. But alas, although they didn't realise it, the workers were chiefly attracted by the priest in him; it was the consecrated man whom they admired. Now he is only one man amongst many and probably they are disappointed in him. In any case it was the end of his glory; there was no point in his remaining any longer in the factory and he took a teaching post in a village where no one knows about his past. And he is now so harsh in his judgment of the Church and so loud in proclaiming his atheism that his very break seems to have become meaningless.

What a pity some officials of the Roman *curia* could not assist incognito at one of these reunions of former priest. Then perhaps they would understand better the serious crisis which so many of the best and most fervent priests face these days.

28th October

I was invited to give a series of lectures in Angers. I confess I was uneasy about the invitation. Catholicism in Angers is notorious for its dogmatist nature and its intolerance of the modern world and of the Catholics who approve of it. Angers is the headquarters of a journal which pretends to represent 'Catholic thought' but in fact represents petty sectarianism. Several of the theologians at Angers university have been heard to speak slightingly about their colleagues at other Catholic universities. The publisher of the review, a denunciatory individual from the dogmatists' camp who has been censured by several bishops, has found in Angers a comfortable perch from which to propagate his views. I was told that the priest from Assy who went to Angers to talk about his famous church was taken to task during a public reunion because, he was told, 'there must be no Catholic art other than that of realism'— i.e. the pious art of Saint Sulpice.

So I was very surprised when I received a warm welcome in Angers and the other towns of the district. Rarely have I addressed such large and friendly audiences. The priests to whom I spoke are not only against dogmatism but they are actually exceptionally broad-minded and interested in modern ideas and abhor both dogmatism and sectarianism quite as much as I do. I know of course that those who invited me and came to see me are precisely the people who *do* share my ideas and that it would be ridiculous to conclude that they are typical of the clergy of Angers. Yet I have spoken these last two weeks to so many priests and laymen that I feel entitled to discount my prejudice about Catholicism in Angers. Even though the dogmatists are busy here and make a great deal of noise I cannot but see that it would be most unfair to take them as typical representatives of the spiritual atmosphere of the town.

1955

15th September

The editor of a Catholic progressive journal said to me the other day: 'You must not be surprised that we never refer to your book *From Karl Marx to Jesus Christ*. However much you tried to be impartial and avoid the traps of cheap anti-communist polemics, the very fact that you have broken with communism and become a Catholic infers that you criticise the former. And although we personally admit that your criticism is justified we feel that for the moment we want at all costs to avoid agreeing with anyone who criticises the communist party or Russia.' This is by no means an unusual point of view. Many Christians who are not communists take every possible care not to offend them. They are afraid of losing touch with the 'masses' whom communism is supposed to represent and of running counter to the 'historical trend' which communism is supposed to embody. This is not a conviction but simply a *complex* in the strictly psychological sense of the word. When men like Mollet or Pinau, leaders of a clearly left party dare attack communism as they attack any other political organisation whose doctrine and tactics they don't approve, our left Christians seem to regard the rebuff as an unpardonable sacrilege. They themselves take good care not to offend the communists and are deeply hurt when, as so often happens, the communists attack the Christians.

If we are to understand this complex it is no use shrugging our shoulders and making fun of it. We must try to understand

186

the working of this type of Catholic mind. The fact that Catholics have for a very long time supported the established order and implicitly or explicitly condoned its injustices resulted in the disastrous separation of the Church from the working masses so deeply deplored by Pius XI. Those Catholics who feel ashamed of past compromise and want the Church restored to the affection of the people instinctively adopt an attitude of psychological compensation. Since at least in France, a large proportion of the people is pro-communist, the Christians, afraid lest they cut themselves off further from them display a spirit of humility and submission which is certainly not consistent with their unorthodox views. The trouble is that communism long ago ceased to be a truly progressive force and has joined the worst type of orthodox ranks. Although the progressive Christians are aware of all this they dare not openly proclaim it for fear of appearing reactionary.

9th October

I had lunch with a group of Dominicans all very active in the field of intellectual apostolate. In the course of the conversation I said how I deplored the Holy Father's custom of passing opinions about all spheres of life, admonishing people like football champions and chemists. Whereas in former times a papal encyclical was a world event the Pope nowadays gives so many addresses and issues so many encyclicals that even fervent Catholics pay little more attention to them than they pay to the Sunday sermon.

On the whole the Fathers agreed with me but one of them remarked that the laity are wrong to complain. They soon protest against an excessive clericalism whenever the Pope or a bishop says something they don't like but they are less quick to applaud the same authority if it says something with which they agree. Basically it is true to say that just as colonialism can only prosper in regions where the people are 'colony minded' clericalism only exists because too many people are 'clerical minded'.

This reminds me of the group of psycho-analysts who complained because the Pope at an audience given to the opponents of their teachings had criticised psycho-analysis so severely that they were afraid he would condemn it altogether. Evidently the Holy Father was not familiar with psycho-analysis and the problems it can stir up and solve. But when the same men themselves went to Rome to take part in a congress they asked to be received in audience by the Pope and made a great thing of the encouraging words he spoke to them, interpreting them as approval of their teaching.

17th October

I have long had a great respect for Mauriac and always read his novels with interest. Although his theory of divine grace with its clear distinction between the natural and the supernatural order never convinced me it nevertheless gave me a useful insight into the working of minds of a certain type.

By nature Mauriac is not left wing and his love of recognition has even placed him in the extreme right wing. Yet his Christian instinct induced him to fight for the oppressed and for justice whenever the need arose in recent years. His sincere faith and his fiery temperament have inspired his language to a level worthy of men like Bloy, Savonarola and the prophets of Israel.

It is all the more irritating to watch him now engaged in furthering the electoral chances of the most despicable of all political parties which is known to encourage corruption and shady practices. If Mauriac wants to vote for this party he is of course free to do so although for a man of his stature it would be more logical to support communism or fascism or the monarchy—in short any cause in which a man can believe. It is terribly difficult to understand why the author who so readily assumes the role of speaker for the Christian conscience should proclaim to the world that only one particular Prime Minister can save France and the Church.

1st December

An Italian weekly, rather on a par with *Paris Match* and *Samedi Soir* has just announced that during a recent illness Pope Pius XII had a vision of Christ. The sensational press obviously couldn't miss such a marvellous opportunity and the published picture of the visionary Pope is a cross between a Holywood star and a notorious murderer.

Some Christians rejoice at the news. They go so far as to say that the supernatural favour accorded to the Pope is a sign that God approves of his actions and doctrinal pronouncements. Some even argue that the vision proves how wise the Pope was to criticise progressive irenism, modern tendencies in philosophy, and theology, evolution, in short anything against which he has ever spoken in the course of the seventeen years of his pontificate.

I am certainly not prepared to support the idea that the vision was a clever political manoeuvre or to describe it as the daydream of a sick old man. From the Christian point of view we have no right whatsoever to doubt the authenticity of the apparition. Considering the Pope's piety it is perfectly feasible that Christ should have appeared to him and nobody is entitled to doubt the perfect sincerity of his testimony.

What is quite intolerable, however, and does much harm to the prestige of the faith, is the noisy publicity given to the vision, to say nothing of the apparently well meant but very grievous blunder committed by the official who disclosed the secret. The Church is quite adamant in its demand that all visions, miracles and private revelations should be treated with the utmost caution. She never approves them before having made long and detailed enquiries—nor does it make any difference whether the visionary is the Pope or the humblest of the faithful. The principle is still the same.

It is horrible to see how the various factions are trying to exploit the supernatural favours accorded to the Pope—all the more so because the Holy Father himself is so touching in his attempt to keep quiet about it. Those who know him well say that he was deeply distressed when he heard that some all-too-zealous admirers were already preparing his future beatification.

And to think the graces conferred on the Holy Father likely to help in the world's conversion one would need to be totally ignorant of modern psychology. For most people today miracles, far from bringing the faith nearer to them, are much more likely to stand in the way of their conversion.

1956

3rd January

A friend of mine, a minister of the Reformed Church said to me the other day 'For years now I have watched a large number of Catholics and noticed how terribly uneasy they feel and I cannot understand why you and people who think and feel as you do, don't leave the Roman Church'.

I would have been hard put to it to try to deny that I have often felt uneasy within the Church or that my uneasiness had not increased in the course of the last few years. At the same time, for myself as well as for my friends, it is out of the question to break away from the Church; the few priests who have effected this divorce have generally finished up by being very sick at heart. I explained to the minister that we believe neither in the teachings of Luthern or Calvin because our faith is the faith of *the* Church. We believe in her, in her teachings and in the efficacy of the sacraments she distributes. Our uneasiness is that of members who see the Church chained too closely to a world of which we don't approve. We are unhappy when we see that she is not sufficiently free to accomplish the mission for which she is called into the world of today and of the future.

Nor is our uneasiness the same as for instance, that of Catholics who, a few years ago took part in the French *move-*

ment. These men accused the Church of meddling in politics simply because they resented that she did not support their own political aims. Many of them out of loyalty to Maurras accepted their dismissal from the Church because they were torn between two irreconcilable loyalties. But our position is totally different. The editor of a progressive paper who was sharply criticised in Rome put the problem very neatly when he said 'Ours is a Catholic action which has sense and meaning only within the Church'. That is the reason why those are wrong who fear—or hope—that the uneasiness from which we suffer and the liberties we take in criticising the Church are sure signs of our imminent apostasy.

Another friend, one of the most talented of young Catholic authors and a recent victim of the dogmatists' vendetta wrote to me: we must at all costs remain loyal to the Church, even if need be in spite of herself.

A group of Catholic students questioned me about the matter of this book which has been advertised as the logical sequel to *From Karl Marx to Jesus Christ*. I tried to explain what had been in my mind when I wrote it; I knew that it would displease many with whom I share the faith in and love for Jesus Christ. Their chaplain concluded: 'You mean that in the first book you told us why you became a communist and why eventually communism disgusted you and you left the party whereas in this new book you tell us what disgusts you in the world of Christians and why, in spite of it, you remain a Christian.' He could not have summed it up better.

In many ways the Christian world seems to me no more attractive than the communist world. Neither corresponds to the idea we are entitled to form of the kingdom of God or an earthly paradise. But the two worlds are fundamentally different from each other.

The communist world is inhuman, degrading and threatening the most genuinely human qualities of man. This is not because, as some dissident communists would have it, Stalin and his followers have betrayed true communism, but on the contrary because they have been only too faithful to the fundamental teaching of Marx and Lenin. Had they not been so loyal the crimes they perpetrated would be less shocking. If we want to remedy the crying abuses of communism we must not try to return to the forgotten origins of the system; we must repudiate these very origins for they are evil.

The situation with regard to the Christian world is totally different. If it is often mediocre, if at times it joins forces with tyrants and oppressors of every description, if it often appears to be sectarian and intolerant, the reason for these defects must not be sought in its loyalty to the gospel of Jesus Christ but precisely in its betrayal of him. If we want to put an end to all that is ugly in the Christian world, to turn its failure into a triumph, we need only return to the Source.